A PRACTICAL GUIDE TO COLLABORATION IN PARTICIPATORY ACTION RESEARCH

Rowena Hay, Susie Hay, and Roger Newton

P

First published in Great Britain in 2026 by

Policy Press, an imprint of
Bristol University Press
University of Bristol
1-9 Old Park Hill
Bristol
BS2 8BB
UK
t: +44 (0)117 374 6645
e: bup-info@bristol.ac.uk

Details of international sales and distribution partners are available at
policy.bristoluniversitypress.co.uk

© Bristol University Press 2026

DOI: 10.51952/9781447364108

British Library Cataloguing in Publication Data
A catalogue record for this book is available from the British Library

ISBN 978-1-4473-6407-8 hardcover
ISBN 978-1-4473-6408-5 paperback
ISBN 978-1-4473-6409-2 ePub
ISBN 978-1-4473-6410-8 ePdf

The right of Rowena Hay, Susie Hay, and Roger Newton to be identified as authors of this work has been asserted by them in accordance with the Copyright, Designs and Patents Act 1988.

All rights reserved: no part of this publication may be reproduced, stored in a retrieval system, or transmitted in any form or by any means, electronic, mechanical, photocopying, recording, or otherwise without the prior permission of Bristol University Press.

Every reasonable effort has been made to obtain permission to reproduce copyrighted material. If, however, anyone knows of an oversight, please contact the publisher.

The statements and opinions contained within this publication are solely those of the authors and not of the University of Bristol or Bristol University Press. The University of Bristol and Bristol University Press disclaim responsibility for any injury to persons or property resulting from any material published in this publication.

Bristol University Press and Policy Press work to counter discrimination on grounds of gender, race, disability, age and sexuality.

Cover design: Liam Roberts Design
Front cover image: iStock/Visual Generation

Dedicated to the memory of Gina Holdsworth who died in 2023. A community leader and activist from Bransholme in Hull, her campaigning resonated both locally and nationally. She believed in the power of PAR and was a brilliant trainer and practitioner.

Contents

List of figures, tables, and boxes		vi
About the authors		ix
Acknowledgements		xi
Book synopsis		xiii
1	Introduction	1
2	Participatory Action Research: where we've been and where we're going	9
3	The process	42
4	The tools	99
5	Reflections on ethics and power	136
6	Conclusion	160
Notes		163
References		164
Index		188

List of figures, tables, and boxes

Figures

3.1	Stages of our Participatory Action Research process	58
3.2	Checklist for assessing Participatory Action Research partnerships	60
4.1	Mapping place	103
4.2	Body map	106
4.3	Timeline	110
4.4	Graffiti wall	114
4.5	H-Form	117
4.6	Causal Impact Diagram	119
4.7	Spider Diagram	123
4.8	Rose, Thorn, Bud	124
4.9	Affinity Clustering	125
4.10	Bean Counter	128
4.11	Criteria Ranking	129
4.12	Impact Matrix	130
4.13	Evaluation Betty	132
4.14	Pizza Pie	134

Tables

3.1	The 'big shifts' in Participatory Action Research	43
3.2	Key differences between teaching and facilitating in Participatory Action Research training	44

Boxes

2.1	Community researcher top tips	19
2.2	Beware of the traps that may be lethal to your Participatory Action Research project	31

2.3	Partnerships, power, and pay	39
3.1	Embracing different learning needs	45
3.2	Asking reflexive questions – seeing ourselves in the research	47
3.3	Safeguarding Camden	48
3.4	Community researcher reflection – sharing findings through song	52
3.5	Navigating strong opinions	56
3.6	Commissioners' reflections – the magic of Participatory Action Research	61
3.7	Flexible, on-the-ground recruitment	62
3.8	Recruitment controlled by gatekeepers	63
3.9	Community researcher reflections – discovering a treasure box of tools	67
3.10	The power of icebreakers that generate laughter	70
3.11	Community researcher reflections – local knowledge in action	77
3.12	Community researcher reflections – stepping into new worlds	79
3.13	Community researcher reflections – discovering confidence in Participatory Action Research	80
3.14	Community researcher reflections – conversations that matter	82
3.15	Analysis isn't for everyone	84
3.16	Brown Bag Lunch on the Aberfeldy estate	85
3.17	Creative collaborator reflections – bringing paintings to life at Petworth House	85
3.18	Participatory Action Research to support action on health and wellbeing at work	88
3.19	Neighbourhood Approaches to Loneliness	89
3.20	A green space with potential, but no action	90
3.21	Better Births – embedding community researchers	91
3.22	Independent evaluation and action learning in the Past for the Present project	93
3.23	The Community Insights Programme – embedding Participatory Action Research in Tower Hamlets	94
3.24	Reflections from a commissioner – upskilling community health champions in evaluative Participatory Action Research	96

4.1	In-situ mapping in Barton upon Humber	103
4.2	Body mapping to explore the realities of social leadership	108
4.3	The power of personal timelines	113
4.4	The power of sharing stories	113
4.5	Uncovering hidden impacts	121
5.1	Community researcher-led ethics	141
5.2	'Feeling at home' – opening conversations on refugee women's access to healthcare in the UK	145
5.3	'Feeling left out' – how professional symbols can undermine participation	147
5.4	Valuing local expertise – lessons from the Single Regeneration Budget era	153
5.5	From community researchers to Participatory Action Research trainers	155
5.6	Small acts of care	156
5.7	Meet the Mighty Mini Research Collective	158

About the authors

Rowena Hay is a social scientist whose work bridges public service, academia, and independent practice. She began her career as a researcher in public service, working on inclusive design initiatives and housing quality research at the House of Lords and the Commission for Architecture and the Built Environment (CABE). Rowena went on to pursue these interests as a researcher at Durham University and the University of Reading, where her work explored mixed-tenure housing regeneration and post-occupancy evaluation. Since 2018, she has directed Shortwork, supporting community researchers to lead projects in areas such as housing retrofit, maternity care, arts programming, and public health. She also delivers training in Participatory Action Research (PAR) and has worked with clients including the Design Council, National Trust, British Red Cross, local councils, national and local charities, and government departments. She is Co-Founder of the Mighty Mini Research Collective, advocating for independent researchers, and is a Clore Fellow and Design Council Expert.

Susie Hay worked in international human rights before joining Hull Developing our Communities (Hull DOC) where she first experienced and learned the power of PAR. She went on to establish Shortwork; as a trainer and practitioner, she worked in the London Boroughs of Camden, Islington, and Tower Hamlets, as well as in Calderdale, Wakefield, and Leeds. She designed and led community networking projects including Local Links in West Yorkshire for the Joseph Rowntree Foundation and Common Purpose, and in Rotherham for COGS public policy consultancy.

Roger Newton was a senior manager in the voluntary and community sector before becoming a community participation consultant. He went on to establish 3Ps – People Promoting

Participation, specialising in community-based PAR techniques. He has designed and led projects in partnership with Northumbria University, the Joseph Rowntree Foundation, the Yorkshire Forward Regional Development Agency, the Local Trust, the Hartlepool Action Lab, and East Marsh United. He has also developed and delivered introductory and more advanced PAR training courses at Northumbria, Leeds Beckett, Huddersfield, and Leeds Universities.

Acknowledgements

In the process of writing this book, we have spoken to and wish to thank many practitioners and inspirational people who have shaped and sustained participatory community research, including Roslyn Abbott, Lora Agbaso, Zac Ahmed, Somen Banerjee, Natalie Baron, John Boyle, Julie Clear, Tony Dearing, Sabina Dewfield, Andy Dorton, Marilyn Doyle, Charlotte Flower, Duncan Fuller, Ingrid Fuller, Kate Gant, John Gaventa, Abigail Gilbert, Romeo Gongora, Kate Guthrie, Laura Hall, Janet Harris, Duncan Hay, Gina Holdsworth, Gill Hughes, Andy Inglis, Janette John, Anita Khalil, Tish Lamb, Rosemary Lamport, Barbara Ludlow, Sybille Manneschmidt, Clare McCarroll, Sabina Mohideen, Tara Okeke, Radhika Puri, Andrew Richardson, John Rowley, Tilly Sellers, Paul Spooner, Linda Tock, and Martin Westerby.

We are grateful to our creative collaborators, whose artistry has enriched this work: Rachel Waite from Holistic Harmonies and Calum Perrin as songwriters and musicians; playwright Theresa Gooda; dancer and performer Rachel Fullegar; poet David Neita; and visual artists Ada Jusic, Sarah Hoyle, Loz Ives, and Kohenoor Kamal.

We also thank commissioners including Kelly Robinson, Jane Findlay, Sue Rhodes, Emily Knight, Helen Grimshaw, Ellie Radcliffe, Susie Crome, Sandra Soteriou, Nicola Donnelly, and Sherrice Weekes, whose partnership has been invaluable.

Special thanks go to Paul Stevens, whose patience, encouragement, and game-changing advice gave us the confidence to write this book as independent researchers, and to the responsive, professional team at Policy Press, including Izzie Green, Ellen Mitchell, and Alexandra Gregory, for their guidance. We are also grateful for the encouragement of Konstanze Spohrer, particularly during the writing retreat at the Gladstone Library – a brilliant place to focus and share ideas with other writers.

We thank Helen Kara, whose writing has inspired us and shown that it is possible to publish outside an institution, and the Institute of Development Studies at Sussex University, for keeping alive the record of PAR in its many guises – particularly the contribution of Robert Chambers and his colleagues, who first introduced us to PAR methodology.

Finally, we thank our family and friends – Howie Miller, Frank Miller-Hay, Lil Miller-Hay, Tom Miller, Dori Miller, Hannah Wilkes, Anna Swain, Gareth Weedall, Katherine Woodfine, Jamie O'Brien, Lynsey Hanley, Jemma Street, Mithila Ramagavigan, Susie Gridley, Alexandra Urdea, Tom Booth, and Chris Hay, with extra gratitude for his careful proofreading – for their inspiration and support.

Book synopsis

This practical guide is designed to equip community researchers, practitioners, and community members with the knowledge and tools needed to successfully engage in Participatory Action Research (PAR) projects. By emphasising the importance of collaboration and equal participation, this book will help you the reader navigate the complexities of working on collaborative PAR projects with a focus on working towards positive change through collective action.

Key topics covered include the following:

1. **Understanding the principles and values of Participatory Action Research:** Exploring the foundations of PAR and learning how to foster trust, inclusivity, and empowerment in your research projects.
2. **Building effective partnerships:** Discovering strategies for establishing strong collaborations between community researchers and other stakeholders, ensuring that diverse perspectives are integrated throughout the research process.
3. **Developing a shared research agenda:** Learning how to co-create a research plan that reflects the needs and aspirations of the community, promoting ownership and commitment from all parties involved.
4. **Utilizing participatory research tools:** Gaining insights into a range of tried and tested research methods that promote active engagement and knowledge exchange.
5. **Navigating power dynamics:** Uncovering strategies for addressing power imbalances and promoting equity in PAR projects, ensuring that all voices are heard and valued.
6. **Sustaining momentum and ensuring long-term impact:** Discovering how to maintain engagement and commitment

throughout the PAR process, and ensuring that the outcomes of your research have lasting effects.

With real-world examples and practical tips, this book is an indispensable resource for anyone seeking to embark on a successful PAR journey. By placing community researchers at the heart of the research process, this guide will help you unlock the full potential of PAR projects and contribute to positive change for individuals, organisations and communities.

1

Introduction

Why this book, and why now?

Our journey with Participatory Action Research (PAR) began in Hull and the East Riding of Yorkshire in the mid-1990s. As people who work in community development, we discovered PAR to be a powerful tool to engage people living and working in extremely deprived and underserved communities, enabling them to identify and address the challenges they faced.

One of early projects involved exploring the causes, consequences, and solutions to high rates of teenage pregnancy in Hull, which were among the highest in Europe at the time. This project proved transformative for both the young people involved and youth workers. By pausing a sense of professional authority and listening to the young people's expertise, everyone learned invaluable lessons and witnessed the immense potential of PAR in building skills of local people, helping them analyse and understand their position in society, and fostering steps towards making positive changes in their lives (Sellers and Westerby 1996, pp 77–80).

Since then, we have implemented PAR in various contexts, addressing numerous topics, and have witnessed the methodology evolve and adapt over time. We have experienced the ebb and flow of the popularity of community-based participatory research, and are thrilled to see a renewed appreciation for the approach(es), including the use of creative tools and methods that once held outsider status, but now enjoy greater prominence in universities, research institutes, and philanthropic organisations (Kara, Gergen, and Gergen 2020; Yang and Dibb 2020; Burns, Howard, and Ospina 2021; Toynbee Hall 2023; Kindon, Kesby, and Pain 2024; UKRI 2024; Young Foundation 2024).

At a time when PAR is regaining favour, we believe it is the perfect opportunity to share our learnings from the margins – from communities like Hull, which is geographically and economically peripheral, to practitioners who may lack a platform to share their experiences and contribute to broader discussions on best practices (Reason and Bradbury 2006, p xxiii).

Our aim is to bring these experiences back from the margins and into view by demonstrating the transformative power of 'handing over the stick' - learning from and working alongside people with deep, local knowledge of a topic or place, and a real stake in ensuring that research leads to some sort of change. (Chambers 1997, p 105).

This book is a distillation of the learning we have gained from working on PAR projects with community researchers across diverse contexts over the last 30 years. Our aim is to share the philosophies and ethical frameworks that guide us, the challenges we have encountered along the way, the pitfalls we have experienced, and practical case studies that bring PAR processes and methods to life through engaging stories. The book is also peppered with stories and reflections from community researchers we have worked with across diverse contexts and subject matters, allowing readers to hear firsthand from those who matter most in our PAR projects.

A key motivation for this book is to provide a toolkit that supports practitioners and community researchers in successfully conducting their own PAR projects. Drawing from our experience providing training to community researchers, community workers, professional researchers, and academics interested in the approach, we recognise the need for a comprehensive guide to the overall process, as well as the practical tools and methods that make PAR projects successful.

In this book, we seek to provide clarity on the refined process we have developed over the years, encompassing planning for PAR projects, recruiting and training community researchers, designing fieldwork, carrying out PAR training sessions, analysing findings, defining recommendations, reporting and sharing findings, and planning for change. We understand the challenges associated with working in groups and facilitating inclusive discussions and processes, and our goal is to address these challenges head-on by providing a resource that shares proven approaches and facilitation techniques.

What is Participatory Action Research?

PAR sits within a suite of participatory and action research methods which centre the involvement of people with lived experience within the research process. The language and terminology to define these approaches vary, and have evolved over time, making it difficult to provide a single, definitive explanation. Participatory methods are applied across various disciplines, including the social sciences, physical sciences, arts, and humanities, with research objectives and techniques deeply rooted in the particular context under investigation (McTaggart 1997; Reason and Bradbury 2006; Israel et al 2013; Fine 2018). The techniques used in such projects are diverse, spanning both quantitative methods (for example, surveys and crowdsourced citizen science) and qualitative methods (for example, interviews, focus groups, deliberative workshops, ethnography, and narrative research) (Aldridge 2016; Lichten et al 2018; Involve n.d.). Additionally, creative methods, such as community-based theatre, photovoice, participatory video, digital storytelling, and arts-based research, are often integrated into participatory projects (Lykes 2006; Mienczakowski and Morgan 2006; Guhathakurta 2015; Kara, Gergen, and Gergen 2020; Fitzgibbon 2022; Brown 2024; Harris 2025).

While participatory methods undoubtedly offer value when incorporated into projects led by professional researchers – for example, through participatory workshops or interviews (Cornwall and Jewkes 1995) – for us, PAR goes a step further by placing community researchers at the heart of the process. Community researchers (also known as peer or citizen researchers) are individuals who are not only members of the community being studied, but also play an essential role in shaping or leading aspects of the research project (Rees et al 2024).

PAR can involve community researchers in different stages of the research process such as commissioning research, refining research questions, gathering data, analysing findings, and disseminating results (McTaggart 1997), with the degree of participation varying across projects. While it is less common for individuals to commission research, community researchers are often engaged as members of advisory boards to shape and scrutinise research projects (Yang and Dibb 2020). In many projects, including our own, community researchers are involved as paid members of the team, receiving training in data collection and analysis, designing the fieldwork, undertaking research, and taking a key role in presenting and disseminating research findings (Guta, Flicker, and Roche 2010).

As previously discussed, a variety of methods are employed in PAR projects to facilitate participation, reflection, and action (Yang and Dibb 2020). Our work embraces a range of qualitative and creative approaches, with a particular focus on drawing and diagramming methodologies (detailed in Chapter 3). These visual techniques serve as a foundation for group-based discussions, analysis, and in-depth conversations surrounding the topic or issue at hand.

Benefits of collaborating with community researchers

By actively involving community researchers, we, like others before us, seek to address power imbalances between researchers and the 'researched' (Wadsworth 1998), professionals and 'ordinary people' (Chambers 1997). This approach moves away from extractive practices, where researchers collect data primarily for their own purposes, often providing minimal benefits to the communities being studied (Kindon 2005; Chilisa 2020; Tuhiwai Smith 2021). Projects led by community researchers can generate insights that reflect participants' experiences, while fostering awareness and understanding among everyone involved (Rappaport 2020; Fals Borda and Rahman 1991).

This collaborative approach can lead to a more nuanced understanding of the research topic, equipping community members with valuable research skills so they can play an active role in the process. Involving individuals with an 'insider view' grants the research project privileged access to knowledge rooted in community membership and lived experiences (Merton 1970). Such participation offers several advantages, including: a deeper understanding of community members' lives, challenges, and aspirations; access to established social networks and community-specific ways of expressing ideas and interacting; more effective communication through shared language and understanding of community dynamics; and a greater vested interest in driving positive changes and ensuring that interventions are appropriate, relevant, and feasible at the local level (Reason and Bradbury 2006; Baker et al 2013; Eng et al 2013).

As is true for other action research methods, PAR should lead to the translation of research findings into practical knowledge that is shared widely and is beneficial to people in their daily lives (Rappaport 2020). Depending on the research context and community needs, action may involve the following:

- Implementing new initiatives or interventions based on research findings to address identified challenges or gaps in services (Adeouye et al 2023).
- Collaborating with policy makers or service providers to drive wider change and integrate research findings into decision-making processes (Tower Hamlets Council n.d.)
- Empowering community members and organisations to engage in advocacy efforts by calling out injustice and inequalities (Stack and McDonald 2018).
- Building and strengthening partnerships between community members and other stakeholders with power to make wider changes to support better lives (Bertrand, Salinas, and Demps 2020).
- PAR also brings about personal changes to community researchers themselves, including valuable work experience, training and opportunities, and increased confidence, self-esteem, and personal agency (Dixon, Ward, and Blower 2019).

While achieving actionable change through PAR can be a significant challenge (Monk 2010), it is essential to remain committed to this aspect of the process (Greenbaum, Jacobs and Zinn 2020). Without action, PAR projects cannot fulfil their potential to bring about better and sustainable services, greater equality, and improved outcomes, however small, for people and communities.

Applications and uses of Participatory Action Research in UK communities

We have worked with community researchers on PAR projects across a range of different topic areas, sectors, places and communities, which include the following:[1]

- **Health, public health and social care:** Involving patients, healthcare providers and carers in identifying systemic barriers to care and co-creating solutions to improve health and social care service delivery. These include projects looking at barriers to cancer screening (Hay 2013), experiences of maternity care (Deng Deng et al 2019), health and wellbeing at work (Hay 2014b), combating Type 2 diabetes (Hay 2014a), community safeguarding (Westerby and Hay 2010), and mental health (Hay 2015).
- **Environmental justice and planning:** Engaging community members in documenting environmental concerns, analysing their impact on health and wellbeing, and advocating for policy changes. These include projects relating to housing (Rezvani et al 2025), planning, and urban design (Hay 2018; Toubajie et al 2024).
- **Community development:** Partnering with residents to identify local needs, assets, prioritise interventions, and implement strategies to enhance quality of life (Hay 2014c). These include community research leading to actions in addressing poverty (Hartlepool Action Lab 2017), and neighbourhood approaches to addressing loneliness (Collins and Wrigley 2014; Hay 2015).
- **Arts, culture and heritage:** Engaging with diverse audience members to understand their experiences, preferences, and barriers to engagement, and using this knowledge to inform programming, inclusion and outreach efforts (Adeouye et al 2023; Carrington et al 2025).
- **Young people:** Often young people's experiences and insights are not included when services are being shaped and solutions

to 'problems' sought. We have found that using PAR and young people themselves as peer researchers is key to finding appropriate strategies to change the quality of their lives (Hay 2008; Newton and Puri 2023).
- **Refugee groups and asylum seekers:** Including projects exploring barriers and solutions to accessing good information on rights and services in the UK as a refugee (Al Hamwi et al 2021).

This book draws on our collective experience of delivering these projects in diverse community contexts. While this book focuses on the UK, we hope that the discussions, learning, and practical tools will also be relevant to practitioners working in other international contexts. Indeed, the methodologies and practical approaches explored here are strongly influenced by the wider PAR field, which crosses national boundaries (see Chapter 2 for more on this).

How to use this guide

This guide is a valuable resource for practitioners of all types looking to apply PAR approaches within their own projects. By offering practical advice, proven methods, and real-world examples, the guide aims to support readers in effectively working together with community researchers to address the unique needs of their communities.

Here is an overview of the guide's structure:

- **Background and history:** Gain a solid foundation in the origins, principles, and evolution of PAR, as well as its various applications across different sectors and contexts.
- **Training and support:** Learn how to equip community researchers with the necessary skills and knowledge to engage in PAR, including training approaches, facilitation techniques, and ethical considerations.
- **Participatory tools:** Discover a range of practical tools and techniques that can be adapted to suit the specific needs of your project, from data collection methods to strategies for fostering collaboration and promoting inclusivity.

- **Ethical questions and reflections on power:** Explore critical ethical considerations in PAR, including issues of consent, confidentiality, and potential power imbalances between researchers and participants. Reflect on strategies for mitigating these challenges and promoting equitable partnerships.
- **Case studies:** Throughout the guide, find examples of PAR projects from various sectors and contexts, offering inspiration and insights into the diverse ways in which PAR can be applied to address complex issues and drive positive change.

By presenting a comprehensive overview of PAR and providing guidance on its practical application, this guide aims to empower researchers and practitioners with the knowledge and confidence they need to embark on their own PAR projects. We encourage you to adapt the strategies and methods presented here to suit your unique context and to continue learning from others in the field as we collectively work towards fostering more equitable and inclusive research practices.

2

Participatory Action Research: where we've been and where we're going

Qualitative research has long played a vital role in uncovering the complexities of human experience. It makes visible the values, relationships, and contextual factors that shape lives – aspects that are often lost in purely quantitative approaches. While numbers can describe patterns, qualitative inquiry helps us understand *why* those patterns exist and *how* they are lived (Alasuutari, Bickman, and Brannen 2008).

In the current research landscape, this human-centred work faces both new opportunities and new challenges. There is a persistent bias towards quantitative approaches in commissioned research by policy makers and third-sector organisations, with qualitative methods often regarded as anecdotal, less rigorous, or used primarily to 'bring to life' numerical findings (Natow 2022). This trend has become particularly pronounced in the context of ongoing austerity and a narrow focus on economic growth in public policy. It is further reinforced by the dominance of evidence-based policy, which frequently positions qualitative approaches at the lower end of 'hierarchies of evidence' due to their perceived lack of generalisability and representativeness (Bennett 2022, p 9; Huff 1991; Murad, Asi and Alsawas 2016; Sturge 2022).

Building on this trend, generative AI technologies now synthesise, and even fabricate, qualitative 'data' at scale (Sutcliffe, Leaver, and Mouameletzi 2025), offering speed and convenience but risking a disconnect from the very people whose lives are being studied. They also risk reproducing hidden biases, stereotypes, and

Western-centric worldviews embedded in large language models (Davison et al 2024; Gibson and Beattie 2025). If research is reduced to text generation and computational pattern spotting, the deeper purposes of qualitative work (such as building relationships, co-learning, and supporting positive social change) are at risk of being sidelined.

PAR stands in sharp contrast to these trends.[1] It is not only a method for generating research findings; it is also a process of collective inquiry and action that depends upon people working together. The value of PAR lies not just in the data it produces, but in the connections made between the people involved, the shared empathy and understanding that is grown, the useful skills and new opportunities developed, and the big and small shifts in power and agency that occur through the process itself.

It may be no coincidence that PAR's renewed visibility and investment have emerged alongside the rise of AI-supported research. Long seen as a niche or 'alternative' approach, PAR is now being actively supported by major funders and institutions. UK Research and Innovation's (UKRI) network of Community Research Hubs (UK Participatory Research Network n.d.), the Local Trust's Big Local programme (Local Trust 2025), the Young Foundation's peer research initiatives (Young Foundation n.d.), and a growing body of participatory work in health, housing, local democracy, and policy development all signal a shift in how policy makers and the research community perceive its value (Yang and Dibb 2020; Toynbee Hall 2021; Chen 2024; Manchester School of Architecture 2025; NHS n.d). PAR is being positioned not just as a methodology, but also as a route to more democratic decision making, stronger evidence for community-led change, and more equitable partnerships between researchers and the public.

Yet for those of us who have worked in this field for decades, this is not a new story. We have seen PAR's rise and retreat before, often shaped by funding cycles, political climates, and shifting institutional priorities. Its history is one of both promise and vulnerability that include moments of flourishing practice followed by periods of neglect, during which valuable knowledge, skills, networks, and relationships have been lost. In its current resurgence, we are reminded of the need to hold on to lessons from past practice and to resist the temptation to treat PAR as a fashionable innovation divorced from its deeper roots.

This is especially important because growing visibility also brings with it new risks. In some cases, PAR and related approaches such as co-production may be co-opted into institutional agendas that value the language of participation, but leave underlying power structures untouched (Dancis, Coleman, and Ellison 2023). Under these conditions, PAR can become a technical tool for consultation rather than a political process addressing social inequality and injustice (Fine and Torre 2021). Its radical potential to redistribute power, challenge inequities, and centre the knowledge of marginalised people is in danger of being diluted, if not actively protected.

If we are to make the most of this renewed interest, we must remember where PAR comes from and what it was designed to do. Its roots lie in traditions of social justice, critical pedagogy, and grassroots activism. We can learn from decades of work in the UK, internationally, and in our own practice about what makes PAR effective, what undermines it, and how it can adapt to new challenges without losing its core principles. In this chapter, we explore those roots, the debates that have shaped the field, and what today's practitioners can draw from both the successes and the shortcomings of the past.

Foundational figures

The current visibility and funding for PAR make it all the more important to revisit the ideas of those whose work underpins its principles. PAR is not new – it has emerged, receded, and resurfaced in different forms over decades. Remembering its roots is not an exercise in nostalgia; it is a way of protecting its real, radical potential.

The following three figures – Paulo Freire, Sherry Arnstein, and Kurt Lewin – worked in very different contexts and eras, but each grappled with the core questions of participation, power, and transformation that remain central to PAR today. Their work offers both practical methods and ethical reminders: that research must be more than a technical exercise; that participation without power is tokenistic; and that cycles of action and reflection must remain grounded in the priorities of those most affected.

In our own practice, we introduce these figures during community researcher training sessions, encouraging participants to identify 'top tips' from each and adapt them to their own projects (see Box 2.1). This process helps new researchers connect their work to a longer tradition of participatory practice – one that is as much about values, principles and ethics as it is about methods. We encourage anyone involved in PAR to do the same – be they professional researchers, academics, commissioners, or community researchers.

Paulo Freire

> Attempting to liberate the oppressed without their reflective participation in the act of liberation is to treat them as objects that must be saved from a burning building.
>
> Freire 2017, p 17

Paulo Freire is widely recognised as a key figure in the development of PAR approaches, alongside a movement of other politically progressive intellectuals who sought to transform research into a tool for consciousness-raising and political mobilisation in Latin America, India, and Tanzania during the 1960s and 1970s (de Silva, Wignaraja, and Rahman 1979; Fals Borda 2006; Swantz, Ndedya, and Masaiganah 2006; Rappaport 2020). Born in Brazil in 1921, Freire's childhood experiences of poverty and hunger profoundly shaped his future work, leaving a lasting impact even after his family's circumstances improved. After studying law at university, he worked as a secondary school teacher before transitioning into adult education in the mid-1940s. Throughout his career, he developed literacy programmes for marginalised groups in Brazil and Chile during a period of political exile (Gadotti and Torres 2009).

Through this work, Freire witnessed the transformative power of education in enabling oppressed individuals to gain agency over their lives by fostering a critical consciousness, or 'concientizacao' (Freire 2017, p 9). Freire felt that by critically examining their social and political circumstances, people are more likely to understand their situation and be better equipped to take action to improve it (Cruz 2013, p 173). In his philosophy, 'liberation' depends on a continuous cycle of critical reflection and action, which he calls 'praxis' (Mayo 2017, p 1946).

For Freire, praxis is central to human existence and freedom because it differentiates humans from animals, which are solely immersed in activity. In contrast, humans can 'emerge from the world, objectify it, and in so doing … understand it and transform it' (Freire 2017, p 98). Denying people the ability to think and act is to deny their freedom and humanity. Enabling praxis therefore forms the basis of freedom and ultimately drives the transformation of societal structures (Freire 2017, p 99; Mayo 2017, p 1946).

The ideas of *oncientizacao* and praxis undoubtedly influence our practice of PAR, even if they are ideals rather than the constant reality. By training people in participatory methods and as community researchers, and supporting them in undertaking research themselves, we seek to elevate the understanding of everyone involved, especially the community researchers participating in our projects. This enables them to gain more knowledge of the issues affecting their communities and the change that might be needed.

In traditional research projects, participants may be involved in research and informed of outcomes, but ultimately, it is through the practice of doing research itself that one gains a deeper understanding of the world (Billies et al 2010). The process of conducting research, engaging with people, and discovering diverse opinions, perspectives, and experiences is the essence of qualitative research that we value. It is the situated knowledge produced through the experience of engaging in fieldwork (Genat 2009). We strive to ensure that our community researchers have an opportunity to experience this always interesting, often challenging, sometimes transformative, and frequently empowering work.

Freire's model of education, presented in his seminal work *Pedagogy of the Oppressed* holds significant relevance to PAR (Freire 2017). His concept of critical pedagogy aims to challenge and deconstruct the traditional power dynamic between teacher and student, where knowledge is merely 'banked' by the teacher and deposited into the students' minds (Freire 2017, p 46). Instead, Freire advocated a more egalitarian approach, viewing the teacher as a facilitator of dialogue and critical reflection rather than an all-knowing authority. In this framework, both teachers and students are considered 'subjects of knowledge', with each contributing valuable experiences and insights to the learning process (Freire 2017, p 53).

This emphasis on valuing the knowledge and experience of all participants is a core principle of our approach to PAR. By questioning and blurring the distinction between 'experts' and 'non-experts', PAR acknowledges that those directly affected by a problem often possess unique insights that can be equally (if not more) valuable than those of academic researchers or professionals (Chambers 1997, p 155). This perspective not only enriches the research process but also empowers participants by validating their experiential knowledge and fostering a sense of ownership over the research process and outcomes; (Ledwith 2016).

Freire's approach continues to shape the way in which research training and community researcher projects are structured. By deliberately working to level power dynamics within these settings, the goal is to create a genuinely collaborative environment in which all forms of expertise are valued equally (Chambers, 1997, p 58).

In subsequent chapters, we will explore the specific techniques used to form working groups that bring together clients, community researchers, and other stakeholder organisations in ways that challenge traditional hierarchies and foster a more democratic, dialogical exchange of knowledge (Rappaport 2020).

Freire's vision reminds us that participation must be inseparable from critical reflection and transformative action. While his focus lay in political education and liberation movements, similar principles were taking shape in a very different discipline: social psychology. There, Kurt Lewin's work laid the foundations for the action–reflection cycles that remain central to PAR.

Kurt Lewin

> It is a type of action-research, a comparative research on the conditions and effects of various forms of social action, and research leading to social action. Research that produces nothing but books will not suffice.
>
> Lewin 1948, p 202

Kurt Lewin, one of the founding figures of social psychology, is often regarded as the originator of Action Research. In 1933, Lewin fled to the US to escape the growing anti-Semitism in Germany and the rise of the Nazi regime (Pasmore 2006). Having worked as an academic in Berlin, he took up a post at the University of Iowa and later at the Massachusetts Institute of Technology (MIT) (Pasmore 2006). During the Second World War, he worked with the anthropologist Margaret Mead on action research studies to make rationed food go further, with housewives themselves involved in exploring the problem and coming up with practical solutions about what could be done (Mead 1943). In the late 1930s, Lewin and his students conducted research in factories, demonstrating that morale and productivity could be improved through democratic participation of workers instead of top-down control, as advocated in the Taylorist model of scientific management (Adelman 1993). The Harwood studies put action research into practice by actively involving workers in exploring problems, making group decisions on how to proceed, and regularly reviewing progress (Pasmore 2006).

The practice of self-reflection, as emphasised by Lewin, strongly influenced the development of what has become known as the action-reflection cycle of research, action, and evaluation, which continues to significantly influence the work of practitioners today (Adelman 1993; McNiff 2013). This cycle serves as an ideal framework rather than a concrete reality in all projects, but PAR practitioners constantly strive to move through each stage: from research (understanding) to action (some sort of change) to evaluation (learning from the impacts of those changes) to research again (McNiff 2013).

In subsequent chapters, we will examine the constraints in implementing the full cycle of Action Research. However, it is important to note that the structure Lewin provided for PAR projects, along with his calls for accountability and a continuous cycle that seeks improvement, remains a key tenet of good PAR practice (Pain et al 2011, p 3). By integrating self-reflection and embracing the iterative nature of the research process, we can better understand and address the complex issues faced by communities and work towards meaningful and lasting change.

Lewin's advocacy for PAR in workplace contexts remains highly relevant to contemporary research, particularly when applied within organisations seeking to improve the processes and services they deliver to individuals and communities. Much of our own work takes place in these settings – including health services, cultural institutions, and local authorities – where embedding PAR can influence institutions that play a significant role in shaping people's lives. Yet this dynamic inevitably raises questions of power: the research questions, agendas, and priorities are often defined by commissioners who control both the resources and the budget, while the needs and interests of the communities involved may differ. This tension is a constant tightrope in our projects, and one we will return to throughout this book.

Lewin's own work faced similar challenges. In the Harwood studies, for example, the focus and desired outcomes of the action research were typically set by factory managers or researchers rather than by the workers themselves. Efforts to improve productivity and staff morale often failed to address the issues of greatest concern to workers, or to confront the broader systemic social, economic, and political barriers that shaped their opportunities. While Lewin's later work with minority groups hinted at a more radical vision of change (Adelman, 1993), the application of action research in these industrial settings fell short of fully realising that potential.

This tension in Lewin's work illustrates a challenge faced by all action research projects: balancing the need to deliver practical, short-term results for clients and funders with the ethical imperative to create research that is genuinely shaped by, and beneficial to, the people most affected. As PAR methods continue to evolve, we must stay alert to these challenges and find practical ways to ensure that participants have a meaningful role in setting priorities, making decisions, and shaping outcomes.

While Lewin's work often centred on organisational change, the same fundamental question – *who holds the power to decide what happens?* – lies at the heart of all participatory research. Sherry Arnstein confronted this question directly, introducing her 'Ladder of Participation' to reveal the gulf between token consultation and genuine power sharing. This is a distinction that continues to shape debates about participation as sharply today as when she first described it.

Sherry Arnstein

> The idea of citizen participation is a little like eating spinach: no one is against it in principle because it is good for you. Participation is, in theory, the cornerstone of democracy – a revered idea that is vigorously applauded by virtually everyone. The applause is reduced to polite handclaps, however, when this principle is advocated by the have-nots. And when the have-nots define participation as redistribution of power, the American consensus on the fundamental principle explodes into many shades of outright racial, ethnic, ideological, and political opposition.
>
> Arnstein 1969, p 216

Sherry Arnstein was a social worker turned public participation manager who worked for the US Department of Housing and Urban Development in the mid- to late 1960s as the chief advisor on citizen participation in the Model Cities programme (Gaber 2019). Drawing upon her experiences, Arnstein developed and published 'A ladder of citizen participation' (1969), a model of democratic decision making that distinguishes between the 'empty ritual of participation' and having the 'real power' needed to effect the outcome of the process (Arnstein 1969, p 216).

In her widely cited article, Arnstein highlights the frustration of community members, or the 'have-nots', who engage in participatory activities without any real sharing of power. She also exposes how public institutions and officials – the 'powerholders' – often deploy participation in its weakest forms, claiming that 'all sides were considered' while maintaining the status quo, ultimately benefiting only a privileged few (Arnstein 1969, p 216).

Arnstein's Ladder of Citizen Participation outlines eight rungs: manipulation, therapy, informing, consultation, placation, partnership, delegated power, and, at the top, citizen control. It remains a powerful analytical tool for designing and evaluating participatory processes across diverse fields, including planning and architecture (Jhun, Shari, and Hassan 2025), health (Dolaty et al 2025), criminal justice (van der Heijden and Collie 2025), and youth and social work (Harju, Bernedo Muñoz, and Tofteng 2024), with thousands of academic citations highlighting its enduring influence (Slotterback and Lauria 2019). The ladder has also inspired other frameworks, such as Hart's (1992) adaptation for children's participation and Rocha's (1997) model emphasising empowerment in planning contexts.

In our work, Arnstein's ladder resonates strongly with community researchers, serving as both a mirror and a compass. It helps us see where a project truly sits and points towards the core principles of PAR (Contreras 2019). While the top rung of full citizen control is rarely achievable, and even pure partnership may not be realistic at every stage, the ladder constantly challenges us to move beyond tokenistic involvement and keep power redistribution in view. During training, we invite our community researchers to reflect on their own experiences of participation – in school, at work, in healthcare, or in planning decisions. Mapping these experiences along a continuum from least to most participatory, using Arnstein's ladder as a visual guide, often sparks moments of recognition and surprise: many realise they have rarely been involved in processes that are genuinely participatory. These reflections make the abstract concept of participation tangible, helping researchers connect theory to lived experience and inspiring a commitment to meaningful engagement in their own projects.

Arnstein's analysis continues to guide our work as facilitators of PAR projects, particularly when commissions come from local government and other public institutions. Her ideals challenge us to reflect on our motivations and ensure that our work is genuinely collaborative, even if we cannot always meet her high standards. Yet, despite her substantial influence, Arnstein herself remains remarkably invisible: finding even a photograph of her proves difficult. This scarcity may reflect, at least in part, her status as a woman and a non-academic at the time. It is a reminder that those who challenge power are not always recognised in the ways they deserve. Her courage and rebellious spirit have left a lasting mark on PAR, and it is vital that we carry this forward.

Box 2.1: Community researcher top tips

Community researchers Adeolu Adeouye, Yaya Clarke, Niki Lavithis, Jo Molina, Nathan Mackie, Celia Morris, Tara Okeke, Calum Perrin, and Magdalen Rubalcava collaboratively developed a set of top tips inspired by the works of Paolo Freire, Sherry Arnstein, and Kurt Lewin during their community research training. These tips served as guidelines for conducting effective, inclusive, and empowering community researchers as part of the Past for the Present project with the Dulwich Picture Gallery.

Paolo Friere:

- Seek to empower community members throughout the research process.
- Meet people where they're at, understanding their unique perspectives and experiences.
- Dismantle traditional views of power, promoting horizontal learning and nonhierarchical structures.
- View the research process as an exchange of knowledge and ideas.
- Promote agency among participants, encouraging active engagement in the research process.
- Think outside the box, embracing creativity and innovation.
- Include research subjects as active participants in the process.
- Set aside ego and redefine the roles of facilitator and participant, embracing a collaborative approach.
- Consider what is relevant and meaningful for the community being researched.
- Consider the larger social context in which the research takes place.

Kurt Lewin:

- Ensure democratic participation, making sure all voices are heard and valued.
- Implement a framework for continuous self-reflection, reviewing, and evaluation.
- Focus on real-life situations and experiences rather than purely academic perspectives.
- Recognise the impact of wider social structures on minority groups and poverty.
- Emphasise group decision-making processes that promote collaboration.
- Leave the hierarchy behind, prioritising nonhierarchical structures in research.
- Involve everyone in problem solving, recognising the expertise of community members.
- Foster happiness and satisfaction by involving all groups in democratic decision making.
- Embrace diverse opinions and perspectives throughout the research process.

Sherry Arnstein:

- Think critically about who the research is being conducted for and why.
- Disrupt the status quo, challenging existing power structures and inequalities.
- Engage the powerless and share power with those participating in the research.
- Reflect on the extent to which participants are genuinely engaged and empowered in the research process.
- Be aware of power imbalances and strive to redistribute power more equitably.

- Avoid using research as a tool for manipulation or to reinforce existing hierarchies.
- Steer clear of leading questions or biased approaches that may skew research outcomes.

Building on the insights of Freire, Lewin, and Arnstein, we see that PAR is fundamentally about reflection, shared power, and meaningful participation. These principles take on new complexity in international development, where cultural, social, and political differences shape how participation is understood and enacted. The following section examines how PAR has been adapted in these contexts, highlighting both the challenges and opportunities of working alongside communities to foster real, sustainable change.

Global perspectives on Participatory Action Research

The previous section explored the philosophical roots of our approach to PAR, drawing on the emancipatory pedagogy of Paulo Freire and the practical frameworks of Lewin and Arnstein. In this section, we turn to the international development arena, where participatory approaches gained global visibility in the late 20th century. This period saw the work of figures such as Robert Chambers and Kamal Kar, who challenged top-down models of rural development and promoted methods that placed the knowledge and priorities of local communities at the centre. While these methodologies and methods remain highly useful and relevant to our work, this period also marked the beginning of debates highlighting the downsides of participatory approaches and the harm caused by their co-option by international development agencies.

As participatory methods became institutionalised within nongovernmental organisations (NGOs), government agencies, and global bodies, they also attracted critiques from feminist, postcolonial, and Indigenous scholars and practitioners. Landmark contributions such as *Decolonizing Methodologies* by Tuhiwai Smith (1999) and later Chilisa's *Indigenous Research Methodologies* (1999) challenge the dominance of Western epistemologies and call for research approaches rooted in the worldviews, values, and priorities of the communities themselves. By questioning whose voices are heard, whose knowledge is valued, and how power operates within participatory processes, these perspectives have profoundly reshaped how PAR is conceptualised and practiced (Patel 2016).

This section begins with the participatory turn in international development in the 1980s and 1990s, and then examines how feminist, postcolonial, and Indigenous critiques have reoriented the field towards more equitable, culturally grounded, and politically conscious practices.

Participatory Action Research in international development

PAR experienced a surge in recognition and adoption in the 1980s, particularly within international development contexts. A pivotal figure in this evolution was Robert Chambers, whose influential book *Putting the Last First* (1983) challenged conventional approaches to rural development. Chambers was deeply influenced by the work of Friere, and advocated for a shift from rigid, top-down approaches to flexible, participatory, and inclusive ways of working (Cornwall and Scoones 2011; Munck 2014). Chambers emphasised the integration of outsider expertise, including academic researchers who 'focus on the why' and development workers who 'focus on the how', with the crucial 'third leg' of insider knowledge from the grassroots (Chambers 1983, p 46):

> The two cultures – academic and practical – share the top-down, core-periphery, centre-outwards biases of knowledge. Both are therefore in danger of overlooking that other approach to understanding from the bottom up, from the periphery towards the core, from the remote towards the central. For the two cultures are cultures of urban-based outsiders. The third culture, of the rural people in a particular place, is the true centre of attention and learning. (Chambers 1983, p 46)

To centre local perspectives, there was a need for new approaches that did not rely on 'overused survey questionnaires', which often reflected outsider concepts, were inaccessible or meaningless to local communities, and reinforced distance between researchers and the people they sought to engage (Chambers, 1983, p 46). Chambers, and his colleagues, championed participatory techniques that emphasised active engagement, listening, and collaborative analysis. These methods were codified in Rapid Rural Appraisal (RRA), incorporating observations, questioning, group discussions, mapping, drawing, and prioritisation workshops (Chambers 1981). Attention to inclusive facilitation, transparency, and the refinement of researcher skills was also central (Chambers 2002). As discussed in the next chapter, combining visual tools with skilled facilitation remains a cornerstone of our PAR practice, with researchers aiming to listen carefully and position themselves as part of the community research team rather than as dominant 'experts' in the process (Chambers 1983, p 200).

In the 1990s, RRA evolved into Participatory Rural Appraisal (PRA) and later Participatory Learning and Action (PLA) as practitioners acknowledged the importance of involving local communities as equal partners in research and development projects. Primarily developed and promoted by NGOs in India, PRA was later adopted by numerous NGOs and government organisations worldwide (Chambers 2012, p 13). This approach valued not only the knowledge of local people but also their capabilities, necessitating a shift from extractive modes of working to more facilitative and participatory methods (Chambers 1997). Consequently, local communities could be empowered to conduct their own analysis, planning, and action (Chambers 1997). Through these developments, PRA in international development grew in prominence, continuously stressing the significance of empowering local communities and appreciating their unique knowledge and experiences. This shift aimed to foster more equitable and sustainable development practices, and to critique the role of the 'development expert and the approach of bureaucratic organisations' (Munck 2014, p 14).

Criticism of participation 'tyranny'

As PRA/PLA gained traction, concerns arose regarding the potential co-option of participatory language by government agencies, NGOs and cross-national bodies such as the World Bank (Gaventa and Cornwall 2006). Critics questioned the authenticity of participatory approaches to development, as discussed in Cooke and Kothari's *Participation: The New Tyranny* (2001). Like Arnstein (1969), they highlighted issues with ritualised participatory processes that manipulate instead of empower participants, and the tendency to treat participation as a technical exercise rather than a way to genuinely hand over decision-making power. (Cooke and Kothari 2001; see also Hickey and Mahon 2004, p 11). Furthermore, focusing too heavily on local issues was criticised because it failed to acknowledge or challenge the fact that power also operates at the national and international levels, including among predominantly Western development agencies (Stokke and Mohan 2001).

Critiques have also targeted the oversimplified view of 'community' in participatory work, which may conceal complex power dynamics and the diverse, sometimes conflicting interests and needs of individuals based on intersectional factors such as gender, age, ethnicity, and class that influence access to power and resources (Guijt and Shah, 1998). These factors also impact group processes and decision making, potentially reinforcing existing hierarchies rather than questioning them (Cooke 2004). From this perspective, Chambers' dualistic view of the world, divided between us and them, high and low status, rich and poor, modern and 'traditional', appears naive (1983, p 173). Having a 'voice' is not enough 'without any effective mechanisms to redress real power differential and inequalities.' (Munck 2014, p14).

Decolonial, feminist, and Indigenous perspectives

Paternalistic approaches to development have also faced criticism, particularly in postcolonial contexts (Baaz 2005). While participatory methods sought to bring local knowledge to the forefront, they often relied on 'outsider' evangelist facilitators, frequently from Western backgrounds, as agents of change (Kapoor 2008, p 63). This has led to critiques of participatory development's position within dominant Western institutions, fitting into broader postcolonial structures rooted in the postwar order (Escobar 2011, p 3). As Kapoor (2008) argues, seemingly progressive initiatives that enhance bottom-up participation may inadvertently mask the continued dominance of Western knowledge, economic, and geopolitical interests.

In response, it is crucial to acknowledge and centre the contributions of non-Western and feminist scholars[2] who have shaped participatory approaches. For example, the prominent feminist scholar Achola Pala (1978) championed co-designed public policies with women, grounded in their own priorities and cultural traditions, and pioneered research on African women conducted by African women. Similarly, the Mexican American Research Association's collaboration with the California Institution for Women in the 1970s (Deeb-Sossa 2019) exemplifies an early form of community-based participatory research led by Chicana women. Addressing the lack of support for women transitioning out of prison, this partnership challenged the monopolisation of knowledge by universities and demonstrated the transformative potential of locally grounded, collaborative research. Contemporary scholars continue this tradition, conducting politically conscious research within Chicanx and Latinx communities to promote health, justice, and wellbeing through locally identified priorities (Deeb-Sossa 2019, p 6).

Indigenous scholarship has further challenged Western epistemic dominance: Tuhiwai Smith's landmark work *Decolonizing Methodologies* (1999) highlights how research has historically served colonial agendas, observing that in the Indigenous world, 'the word itself, "research", is probably one of the dirtiest … It stirs up silence, it conjures bad memories, it raises a smile that is knowing and distrustful' (Smith, 1999, p 1). Bagele Chilisa's *Indigenous Research Methodologies* (2012) complements this work by demonstrating how colonial research historically served the interests of colonisers and continues to do so in an era of globalisation. Chilisa explores the meaning of postcolonial Indigenous research, including its methodologies, philosophies, and worldviews, while critiquing traditional methods such as conventional interviews for their limitations in capturing Indigenous perspectives. Importantly, she highlights participatory research approaches that 'enable oppressed and disempowered groups to collectively share and analyse their knowledge, life experiences, and conditions, and to use Indigenous knowledge as a basis to plan and to act' (p xvii).

Building on these foundational critiques, more recent methodological work, such as *Arts-Based Methods for Decolonising Participatory Research* (Seppälä, Sarantou, and Miettinen 2021), explores creative strategies that decentralise researcher authority, amplify marginalised voices, and allow alternative forms of knowledge expression often excluded from conventional techniques. Similarly, Toliver (2021) highlights the value of Black storytelling as a research method, demonstrating how narrative and oral histories foreground community experiences, challenge dominant discourses, and create space for collective memory and resistance.

Feminist, decolonial, and Indigenous perspectives highlight that the ethical and political challenges in participatory research do not disappear simply because they are acknowledged. As Tuhiwai Smith (1999) and Chilisa (2012) emphasise, colonial research practices have not ended; processes of colonisation persist in contemporary global contexts, including ongoing threats to Indigenous lands, rights, and worldviews. Top-down approaches remain the norm in many development and research initiatives, and participatory research continues to focus disproportionately on poor or marginalised communities who are arguably 'overstudied', while attention to the structures of power and the actions of the powerful is often neglected. Engaging critically with these perspectives calls for constant reflexivity about whose knowledge is prioritised, whose voices are amplified, and whose interests are being served.

One way to make these critiques operational is to use them as a lens for evaluating PAR projects. For example, researchers might ask the following questions:

- Who defines the research agenda, and whose knowledge is prioritised?
- Are local communities genuinely co-leading the research or are they primarily subjects of study?
- How are structural inequalities and power relations addressed within the project?
- Are Indigenous or marginalised knowledge systems and methodologies respected and integrated?

- Does the research challenge or reinforce existing hierarchies, both locally and globally?
- How are benefits, recognition, and opportunities for agency distributed among participants?

Using such questions as a guide can help ensure that participatory approaches move beyond superficial inclusion towards genuinely equitable, accountable, and ethically informed research practices. These questions guide our PAR work within UK community development, a distinctive context that we will explore in more depth in the next section.

Participatory Action Research in the UK: history and critical reflections

This section documents the adoption and adaptation of PAR from international development contexts into the UK, with a particular focus on Hull and the East Riding of Yorkshire. We present this history based on our own experience, as much of this work has not been fully recorded elsewhere. By situating PAR in its local and national context, we can trace both its potential and its challenges in addressing social inequality and as a tool for community development.

Participatory appraisal in UK community development: the case of Hull and the East Riding of Yorkshire

In the UK, PRA and LA were adopted under the broader framework of Participatory Appraisal (PA). During the 1990s, these approaches were implemented as community development tools, particularly in communities experiencing multiple forms of deprivation. The agents for this change were often people who had experience of using PRA/PLA in developing countries and who saw the method(s) as pertinent to the UK context. Andy Inglis in Scotland in the early 1990s was delivering PA training to workers and also implementing projects in rural development in particular, while the Institute of Development Studies at the University of Sussex, where Robert Chambers was based, was another key hub for sharing experience and information (Thompson and

Cannon 2023). Participatory Practitioners for Action (PPfC), funded by Oxfam's UK Poverty Programme, brought together many practitioners from across the UK to share their learning and to address questions and concerns arising from their work (Rowley, Doyle, and Hay 2013, pp 92–96). The proliferation of sticky notes and dots grew and grew, and 'handing over the pen' replaced 'handing over the stick', with issues drawn on flipchart pads, not on the ground (Chambers 1997).

As an example, we cite here work that took place in the Hull and the East Riding of Yorkshire, not because it is the 'best' or only work, but because this is the history that we as authors of this book are most familiar with. From 1994 to 2002 onwards, community-based work in disadvantaged areas burgeoned in the UK with the availability of significant funding from governmental sources, notably the Single Regeneration Budget (SRB) through the Regional Development Agencies, and other government initiatives like Housing Action Trusts, New Deal for Communities, and the establishment of Children's Centres with communities at their heart. These initiatives placed a strong emphasis on the role of community development and community members themselves in making change, and the promotion of partnership (co-production) across government agencies and NGOs. In addition, to support training, the availability of significant funds for adult learning resulted in the growth of both PA projects and PA training across the UK. Hull and the East Riding benefited from this, with Hull itself, an almost forgotten location of post-industrial deprivation, out on a limb on the east coast of England, receiving substantial resources through Yorkshire Forward for renewal through its regeneration company, Hull CityVision.

The catalyst for the use of PA in the area was a project that used teenage peer facilitators trained in PA to investigate barriers to improving adolescent sexual health at a time when Hull had the highest rate of teenage pregnancy in the UK. This work was led by Tilly Sellers, who had worked overseas with Robert Chambers (Sellers and Westerby 1996). This project was a partnership endeavour involving Hull Royal Infirmary's Department of Gynaecology, the University of Hull Department of Health and Primary Care, and local voluntary sector and community organisations. Training was key, with Andy Inglis coming from

Scotland to deliver the first training course in the area specifically for this project. The success of this project and exposure of people to the power of PA led to the adoption of PA by a plethora of local community organisations and other agencies, and in hundreds of community members and workers being trained and accredited in the method over the period of six years. Together they formed the Hull and East Yorkshire Participatory Appraisal Network (HEYPAN). This network was endorsed and supported by the Institute of Development Studies, the University of Hull Centre for Lifelong Learning, PeaNut at Northumbria University, as well as by Yorkshire Forward, the regional Development Agency for Yorkshire and the Humber. Oxfam's UK Poverty Programme (led by Charlotte Flower, who herself trained in PA in Hull) further facilitated the use and promotion of PA in the context of urban and rural poverty across the country (Oxfam 2001).

Together with the University of Hull Centre for Lifelong Learning, further accredited courses were developed by HEYPAN, including Train the Trainer for PA, and an advanced course in PA practice. People came to Hull to access training, including from overseas for the Advanced course, and HEYPAN people delivered training across the country and beyond. With endorsement from the Institute for Development Studies (IDS) and connection with others like Oxfam, HEYPAN and its constituent members found a source of income from running the courses in order to fund more PA work in the area.

Early projects resulting from this work in Hull and the East Riding showcased the potential of PA in engaging local communities and fostering bottom-up, grassroots development, as did the accredited training that HEYPAN provided both locally and nationally. Contexts for projects in the area included Young People, Quality of Life, Healthy Living, Sexual Health, Drugs, Domestic Violence, Community Safety, and Whole Systems Events. These initiatives demonstrated how participatory approaches could help address the unique challenges faced by disadvantaged communities in the UK, while also empowering residents to take an active role in shaping their neighbourhoods. Often a PA project provided the evidence and baseline information required for accessing funding, for example, from the National Lottery and the SRB. Key to this was recognising the importance of local knowledge and expertise, as well as the need for inclusive methods that could involve diverse community members (then known as the 'hard to reach') and not just the 'usual suspects' who already have a powerful voice. By prioritising the views and attitudes of local people, PA enabled more effective and context-specific responses to pressing issues in deprived areas.

However, we are mindful of the problematic aspects of New Labour's approach to regeneration and their vision of 'community' as the cornerstone of this work. Programmes such as the New Deal for Communities positioned 'the community' as the natural and unquestioned locus for tackling deprivation. While this emphasis appeared progressive, it often masked deeper structural issues, such as deindustrialisation, welfare retrenchment, and persistent regional inequalities, by shifting responsibility for regeneration onto residents themselves (Imrie and Raco 2003; Amin 2005). Participation (including PAR methodologies) risked being instrumentalised to deliver centrally defined targets and performance outcomes rather than enabling meaningful redistribution of power. In this sense, the celebration of 'community' under New Labour could be experienced by communities and third-sector organisations as both a resource and a burden: on the one hand, it opened up possibilities for residents to have a voice, secure funding, and influence decision making; on the other hand, it reinforced stigmatising narratives that positioned disadvantaged neighbourhoods as problems to be fixed.

Against this backdrop, community sector organisations and practitioners in Hull and beyond turned to PA as a way of resisting these narratives and reclaiming the value of local knowledge. Unlike top-down models of participation tied to government agendas, PA emphasised the value of local knowledge and sought to build agency among residents themselves. While not always easy (see Box 2.2), importantly, the adoption of PA, which places trust in and respects local people's knowledge and expertise, ran counter to dominant narratives about working-class communities, particularly those in the deindustrialised north of England, living in stigmatised housing estates (both high and low rise) on the outskirts of cities, such as Bransholme and Orchard Park in Hull. Residents of these areas were often labelled as 'skivers' and framed as responsible for societal problems through a so-called 'culture of poverty', rather than acknowledging systemic factors such as deindustrialisation and economic inequality (Valentine and Harris 2014; Jones 2020). PA offered a means to challenge these negative narratives by empowering local communities to document and address their own issues. In Hull, PA initiatives engaged residents in identifying local challenges and co-creating solutions, fostering a sense of agency and pride. These projects have not only generated valuable insights into the lived experiences of Hull's residents, but are also a way to counteract the dominant narratives that stereotype and marginalise them.

> **Box 2.2: Beware of the traps that may be lethal to your Participatory Action Research project**
>
> 1. Calling it 'research' or 'consultation' can completely put off local people who may say, as they did in Hull, 'we've been consulted to death here ... nothing ever happens'. Call the process something else.
>
> 2. The 'real wreckers', sometimes the (self-appointed) leaders who say they speak for the community when in fact they only speak for themselves, and prevent others from having a voice. Have your 'anti-saboteur' tactics at the ready (see Chapter 3 for more on this).
>
> 3. Academics and/or professionals who come into communities to include local people in spatial planning and bring flat plans as the tool. Think again – maybe Duplo Lego might work better.
>
> 4. 'Postcode assumptions' can lead to misconceptions – for example, young people written off for lack of aspiration or academic achievement are often original thinkers with enterprising ideas and who know how things should be run.
>
> 5. The local press who like a story about communities and will run with anything negative that might be fed to them. Have your press release ready.

> 6. Powerful people and institutions can be very conservative and dismiss what might seem outlandish ideas for change. Local people, on the other hand, can often come up with and be inspired by wacky or seemingly pie-in-the-sky suggestions.

As well as significant funding investment in Hull and other areas, active pathways existed, enabling communities and the third sector to influence central government, such as through Community Matters with its regional networks and the Community Development Foundation. Both these organisations engaged directly with the government, and indeed personnel moved from these organisations into the Active Communities Unit at the Home Office. Community members and other representatives from Hull regularly gave evidence to the All Party Parliamentary Group on Poverty, while the Community Development Foundation and Community Matters held conferences jointly with local groups in Hull. Thus, there were active conduits for money to be devolved and for power, influence, experience, and ideas to 'trickle up'.

With the financial crash in 2008 and subsequently with the change of government, the climate changed radically, with funding drying up and the Regional Development Agencies being abolished. The Coalition government's Spending Review in 2010 brought in huge cuts to funding and austerity took over. Both Community Matters and the Community Development Foundation reduced their activities and eventually closed in 2016. These cuts had a devastating effect on the community and voluntary sector, which was felt unevenly across UK communities, with those in more deprived local authorities, like Hull, suffering most due to their greater dependency on statutory funding (Jones et al 2015).

Participatory Action Research in an age of austerity: a dispersed field

The financial crisis of 2008 and the election of the Coalition government in 2010 marked a sharp decline in central government funding for participatory approaches in the UK. Although the language of 'community' persisted through David Cameron's 'Big Society' agenda, which promised to decentralise power and empower local residents by rolling back the role of the state, the resources to realise this vision did not match the rhetoric (Ishkanian and Szreter 2012). For many, this could have signalled the end of a thriving period of PAR. Yet, while formal support dwindled, the method survived and, in places, adapted to the new realities of austerity. This period saw PAR becoming more dispersed, with activity sustained through three main strands: practitioner-led freelance and contract work; philanthropic and NGO support; and institutional academic hubs.

While funding dried up, in the case of the HEYPAN practitioners, many carried on with their work as their 'day jobs' took them to other parts of the country; they became independent PA practitioners, often working together on projects arising from their work or as freelance practitioners and trainers. For example, work grew from freelance projects undertaken by Martin Westerby in the London Boroughs of Camden and Tower Hamlets led to practitioners taking many commissions for both training and community research. In Camden, for example, PA became embedded in the work of the Parent Council led by Barbara Ludlow, and issues like safeguarding (relating to families and to young people), and families' experience of education for children with special needs. This led to further work including a Quality of Life PA project in South Hampstead Community Centre (SHAK). The authors were commissioned by the Assistant Chief Executive's Department of Camden Council in 2014 to recruit and train a large team of local people to undertake engagement with people in the borough to access views about the Council's services. Barbara Ludlow, Sandra Soteriou, and Anita Khalil from Camden in particular have gone on to embed PA practice extensively in the work they carry out in communities in Camden and beyond – Khalil as leader of a team of Neighbourhood Health Champions in the borough.

A similar growth in PA projects took place in Tower Hamlets from 2010 to 2018 principally commissioned by the Council's Public Health Department, all involving training local people in PA who then engaged with their fellow residents on key issues including healthy eating and active lifestyles, barriers to accessing cancer screening services, high rates of type 2 diabetes in the Borough, community asset mapping and the rising epidemic of loneliness. Word spread, and PA projects were commissioned by other organisations including Providence Row (experiences of people with dual diagnosis – mental health issues and drug addiction – in Tower Hamlets, looking at ways in which they might move forward in their lives) and with Poplar Housing and Regeneration Community Association (HARCA) estate workers looking at health and wellbeing in the workplace. This work has also been bolstered by East London institutions such as Toynbee Hall, which have a long supported community-rooted PAR projects, building on a tradition of social-oriented and participatory research projects to tackle poverty and inequality in London's East End (Toynbee Hall 2023).

A great many training courses in PA (and the train the trainer and advanced courses) were delivered by the PA practitioners across the country, including (to name but a few) in Wakefield (for community health workers), Todmorden (Upper Calder Valley) with young people in the Futurejobs project, Hastings (for residents and workers involved in the Community Trust), and Castleford (for users and workers of the Drugs Service), and with the SOS Gangs Project at the St Giles Trust in South London.

Simultaneously, pockets of institutional support for participatory research emerged, with the Joseph Rowntree Foundation (JRF) serving as a notable example. The JRF has long advocated for participatory approaches to poverty research, drawing early lessons from the institutional development literature and addressing challenges in the emerging UK research field (Bennett and Roberts 2004). These challenges include determining 'who' to involve, navigating power differences within 'poor' UK communities, acknowledging that a cosy community consensus cannot be assumed, and recognising that participation is neither cost-free nor compulsory for members of a community. The JRF emphasised the need for tailored support and information to facilitate involvement, which will vary depending on individuals' capacity and willingness to participate. Additionally, questions on 'how' individuals should be involved were raised – whether as participants or having more control over the process, including interpreting data using their insider experiences (Bennett and Roberts 2004). The JRF led a number of PAR projects, including a study focusing on community perspectives on loneliness (JRF 2013), and the Hartlepool Action Lab, launched in 2016, which was expressly designed to help reduce poverty in the area, with solutions designed and funded based on a piece of PAR undertaken by a group of community members in the area (*Hartlepool Mail* 2016; Skelton 2024). The Hartlepool Action Lab in particular was an innovative approach to participatory grant funding, rooted in the needs of local people, with the evidence base and action plan facilitated through PAR.

Durham University's Centre for Social Justice and Community Action (CSJCA) has played a pivotal role in fostering university–community-based action research collaborations. Established in 2011, the Centre became a key resource for developing practical toolkits and ethical guides that support high-quality PAR work. With a focus on interdisciplinary research, the Centre was set up to promote and develop research, teaching, public engagement, and staff development, both within and outside the University. It emphasised the importance of active partnership and collaboration between researchers, community activists, and grassroots organisations. The Centre's work has spanned various topics, including asylum seekers' rights, financial inclusion, racism, and community-led heritage and environmental development.

The CSJCA became particularly renowned for its contribution to the ethics and methodology of PAR. Under the leadership of academics such as Sarah Banks (Banks and Brydon-Miller 2018), the Centre developed ethical guidelines that were adopted worldwide, including by the International Collaboration for Participatory Health Research (ICPHR 2022). These guidelines set out clear but adaptable principles for collaborative community-based PAR projects, including mutual respect, equity and inclusion, democratic participation, active learning, making a difference, collective action, and personal integrity (Centre for Social Justice and Community Action 2022b, pp 10–11). Alongside practical steps and examples of how these can be operationalised in research preparation, planning, working agreements, data generation and analysis, and impact sharing (Centre for Social Justice and Community Action 2022b, pp

12–18; Durham Community Research Team 2022), the Centre's commitment to understanding the nature of impact in PAR led to the establishment of the Participatory Research Innovation and Learning Labs (Centre for Social Justice and Community Action n.d.), further strengthening the connection between research and action for social justice. The Centre was also pivotal in founding the UK Participatory Research Network, a group of practitioners, academics, and community partners from different sectors who embrace the philosophy, principles, and potential of participatory research.

This post-2008 landscape was marked by both resilience and fragility. While PAR practice persisted and in some cases flourished, it often did so through fragmented, short-term, and project-based arrangements. The dispersal of the field made it adaptable but also more precarious, with work shaped by the agendas and funding cycles of commissioners. Austerity also heightened the challenge of ensuring that participation was genuinely community-led rather than extractive. In this context, the commitment of practitioners, the strategic role of philanthropic trusts, and the anchoring presence of academic hubs were critical to keeping the field alive.

Participatory Action Research today

In recent years, PAR has experienced a marked resurgence, with increasing recognition from both institutions and communities of the value of participatory approaches. This renewed interest reflects a growing emphasis on bottom-up methods and locally informed democratic decision making, particularly in a context where many citizens feel disconnected from national politics and formal decision-making processes (Bennett 2022). Participatory approaches allow communities to identify priorities based on local knowledge, address both social and environmental challenges in their immediate surroundings, and develop context-specific strategies that are meaningful, sustainable, and socially connected. They also represent a moral and operational imperative: to ensure that services and policies work for the people they are designed for, to give voice to those often excluded, and to increase awareness of the unintended exclusionary impacts of top-down approaches to policy making and public service design. Examples of contemporary participatory approaches include citizens' assemblies (Ehsassi 2025), user-centred design (Folan 2024), patient panels in the NHS (National Health Service England 2017), citizen science (Marshall n.d.), and participatory grant-making initiatives (National Lottery Community Fund 2025).

Within academia, there has also been a marked upsurge in engagement with participatory methodologies. Over the last two decades, participatory and co-produced research approaches have expanded significantly across the social sciences, health research, environmental studies, heritage and the arts (Aldridge 2016; Warwick-Booth, Bagnall, and Coan 2021; Stuart and Maynard 2022; Ledwith and Springett 2022; Howard and Tadros 2023; Pahl, Steadman-Jones, and Vasudevan 2023; University of Oxford n.d.), with journals dedicated to participatory methods,[3] research funders increasingly framing calls in terms of co-production and community partnership (UKRI 2025), and Research England's Participatory Research Funding, which has supported higher education providers to offer specific funding pots to support participatory research within their institutions (University of Liverpool n.d.). The proliferation of conferences, networks, and methodological handbooks reflects this trend, as participatory approaches are increasingly viewed not only as valid but also as essential for producing socially relevant and impactful knowledge (Burns, Howard, and Ospina 2021; Stoecker and Falcón 2022). The increased importance of research impact, driven by initiatives such as the Research Excellence Framework (REF) and funders' emphasis on demonstrable societal benefit, has further incentivised the adoption of participatory approaches. By engaging communities directly in the research process, PAR offers a clear pathway to producing knowledge that is both academically rigorous and socially relevant, supporting case studies that illustrate real-world impact. Alongside the expansion of participatory methodologies, there has been greater emphasis on, and resourcing of, staff whose role is to engage the public in research. Universities increasingly employ public engagement specialists, community liaison officers, and knowledge exchange staff to support co-produced research and participatory initiatives.

Concurrently, the work of the Young Foundation, the Centre for Community Studies, and the Local Trust has further contributed to the re-emergence of PAR. The Local Trust supported a number of PAR projects to develop the evidence base for local initiatives funded as part of the Big Local funding programme which provided long-term funding for community-led projects across 150 areas of England (Local Trust 2015). The Young Foundation's rediscovery of its roots through the Centre for Community Studies reflects a broader institutional commitment to participatory approaches, recognising the importance of local knowledge and expertise in shaping effective policy and practice (Young Foundation n.d.). Their Peer Research Network offers training, case studies, and a set of ten principles for peer research, adapted from the European Citizen Science Association's guidelines and UK practice reviews. These principles stress active community involvement in knowledge creation, ethical awareness (including intellectual property and confidentiality), collaboration between peer and professional researchers, and the importance of involving peer researchers across all stages of the process, with transparent communication about impacts and legacies (Young Foundation 2024b).

Perhaps the clearest sign of PAR's growing legitimacy is the recent UKRI investment in a network of eight Community Researcher Networks across the four nations (Saunders, Goulden, and Chapman, 2024). Administered by the Young Foundation, these five-year partnerships bring together voluntary sector organisations, academic institutions, and statutory bodies to address locally defined priorities. Topics range from youth voice in Staffordshire to mental health in Moray, to rural access to health and social care in County Durham. This funding not only challenges earlier scepticism about PAR's rigour but also begins to create an infrastructure for career pathways and long-term development for community researchers.

As PAR continues to gain traction, it is essential to learn from past experiences and maintain a critical perspective on its applications. PAR's rich history serves as a foundation for reflecting on the field's evolution, past and present challenges, and future trajectories. Issues such as the persistence of colonialism, extractivism, co-option, and the implications of

PAR's increasing popularity among funders and universities must be addressed (Centre for Social Justice and Community Action 2025). To ensure effective university-community collaborations, critical questions must be explored, including the importance of transparent funding arrangements and the need for deep thinking around 'where the money goes' (see Box 2.3) (Martikke, Church, and Hart 2015). This really matters in a context where the cost of living crisis and cuts to the welfare system are pushing more and more households into poverty (JRF 2025), leaving community and voluntary sector organisations to shoulder a growing burden of support. Power dynamics also warrant careful consideration, emphasising the necessity to avoid a salvation mentality and focus on long-term sustainability of PAR initiatives. This entails genuinely questioning where expertise lies and promoting collaboration that works together on shared problems, issues, and research questions rather than assuming that professionals 'know best' (Sathorar and Geduld 2021). Ethical considerations beyond the traditional 'tick-box' approach should be incorporated to encourage authentic engagement and avoid perpetuating power and resourcing imbalances (see Chapter 5 for deeper reflections on the themes of ethics and power).

> **Box 2.3: Partnerships, power, and pay**
>
> In a collaborative project involving a small community arts organisation, a major university, and ourselves, tensions arose around pay, expertise, and the distribution of benefits. We were paid a middle amount, academic partners received the highest rates, and community partners the least. When the day rates were revealed, community partners were understandably angry, feeling that their time and expertise were valued the least of everyone involved.
>
> At the same time, academic partners believed they were bringing professional expertise and knowledge to the project and felt frustrated that this contribution was not fully recognised or appreciated by the community organisation. Conversely, the community organisation felt that their own

expertise and experience were entirely unacknowledged, creating a sense of inequity and undermining trust.

This situation highlighted several recurring issues in PAR:

- Unequal recognition of expertise: Universities assumed they brought the primary expertise, leaving community organisations feeling patronised and undervalued.

- Imbalanced remuneration: Community organisations are too often expected to participate without fair pay, even though their knowledge and networks are critical to the project's success.

- Career versus community benefit: Research outputs frequently advance academic careers more than they support, elevate, or sustain community initiatives.

- Sustainability concerns: Once the project ends, academics may move on, while community organisations continue to shoulder ongoing responsibilities and relationships.

Lessons learned:

1. Ensure transparent and equitable funding arrangements, making day rates and budget allocations clear to all partners from the outset.

2. Recognise and value community expertise on an equal footing with academic knowledge.

3. Prioritise long-term sustainability, planning for ongoing support and benefits for community organisations.

4. Consider the ethical and operational implications of participation, ensuring that projects genuinely support community work while also advancing academic agendas.

The renewed visibility of PAR offers a chance to consolidate and deepen the field, but only if it stays true to the principles that have sustained it through more precarious times. The lessons from its post-2008 survival are instructive: adaptability, cross-sector alliances, and practitioner commitment will remain as important as formal funding. By carrying forward these lessons while responding critically to new challenges, PAR can continue to foster equitable, collaborative, and impactful research, rooted in the knowledge and agency of the communities it serves.

Conclusions

The history of PAR reveals a constantly evolving field shaped by pioneering thinkers such as Paulo Friere, Sherry Arnstein, and Kurt Lewin, and enriched by methods developed in PRA and PAL within international development. Over time, PAR's value in generating locally grounded, socially relevant knowledge has gained increasing recognition – yet its trajectory has also been marked by persistent challenges, including power imbalances, co-option, and paternalistic or colonial overtones.

Feminist and postcolonial critiques remind us that reflecting on our own assumptions, recognising our standpoint, biases, and privileges, and attending to the politics of knowledge are crucial for maintaining PAR's democratic aims. The experiences in Hull, and the wider contraction of funding after the 2008 financial crisis, underline the necessity of building resilient infrastructure to support PAR in both lean and abundant times.

Emerging commitments from UK research councils, philanthropic trusts, and sector bodies suggest that such infrastructure is now within reach, offering scope to strengthen and embed community-led research as a legitimate, rigorous, and impactful approach to addressing complex challenges.

Moving forward, the task is not only to expand PAR's reach but also to ensure that it remains true to its roots: inclusive, empowering, and critically self-aware. This means resisting co-option, sustaining deep partnerships, and centring the expertise of those most affected by the issues at hand so that PAR continues to serve as a catalyst for collective inquiry and transformative action.

3

The process

In this chapter, we set out the PAR process, exploring its core ethos and the various stages involved. From recruiting community researchers to data analysis and reporting, this chapter serves as a comprehensive guide to understanding and implementing a PAR project.

We begin with an overview of the ethos that frames our projects, discussing the fundamental principles and values that underpin this collaborative approach to research. Building on Lewin's cycle of reflective action (introduced in Chapter 2), we present a clear process outlining the stages of a typical PAR project.

To gain a deeper understanding of the tools and techniques employed, readers are encouraged to read this chapter alongside the following one (Chapter 4), which provides an in-depth exploration of the specific methods utilised during fieldwork, analysis, and feedback. By thoroughly exploring each stage of the PAR process, this chapter equips readers with the knowledge and tools necessary to successfully implement PAR in their own research.

Ethos and approach

Before delving into the specific steps and techniques involved in a PAR project, it is essential to understand the ethos behind this approach and how it differs from other qualitative research methods. PAR is not inherently superior to more traditional approaches but serves a unique purpose, making it a powerful tool

Table 3.1: The 'big shifts' in Participatory Action Research

Traditional research	Participatory Action Research
Teaching	Facilitating
Top-down	Bottom-up
Extracting	Empowering
Closed	Open
Text-based	Visual and Verbal
Individual	Group

Note: This table sets out a series of big shifts needed in PAR as adapted from Robert Chambers (1997, p 154).

when conditions are right. Keeping in mind Sherry Arnstein's ladder of citizen participation (see Chapter 2), it is crucial for all parties to recognise the project's purpose and ensure its impacts are tangible, measurable, and co-owned by all participants. While nuances will be explored further in later chapters, the following guiding principles illustrate the core ethos underpinning our PAR projects.

To highlight these distinctions, and taking the lead from Chambers (1997), we compare PAR with traditional social scientific research methods, such as structured interviewing, focus groups, and surveys. Although this comparison is simplified, it defines the unique characteristics of PAR. For us, the difference PAR makes can be defined as a set of 'big shifts' in behaviours and attitudes summarised in Table 3.1 above and explored in more depth in the following sections.

The big shifts

From teaching to facilitating

Inspired by Paulo Freire's philosophy, we, as PAR practitioners, distinguish ourselves from traditional educators by shifting our role from teachers to facilitators. This shift is vital, as it recognises that participants are not passive recipients of knowledge, but active contributors with valuable experiences and insights. The

Table 3.2: Key differences between teaching and facilitating in Participatory Action Research training

Teaching	Facilitating
Takes their own knowledge as a starting point.	Takes the knowledge of the group as a starting point.
Follows a pre-defined curriculum.	Addresses issues identified by the group and adapts to their needs, knowledge, and interests.
Presents new information from the front of the room.	Uses practical and participatory tools, including group discussions and activities in which everyone takes part.
Focused on making sure students get the answer 'right'.	Actively seeks out different views and answers.
Works at a distance and has a higher status.	Works in collaboration as an equal.

Source: Adapted from Clarke, Blackman, and Carter (2004)

key differences between facilitating and teaching are summarised in Table 3.2.

In our approach, you rarely see us at the front of the room, presenting or teaching in the conventional sense. We try to avoid PowerPoint presentations at all costs. Instead, we are down in the thick of things, sitting around tables, talking with participants, and helping move the process along. Our role is to provide structure and support, enabling people taking part to explore topics, tools, and techniques on their own terms (Cornwall and Jewkes 1995; Kindon, Pain, and Kesby 2010). You might also find us on the sidelines, allowing the process to unfold, stepping in only when necessary. Our role as facilitators is not to dominate the conversation or dictate outcomes, but to create an environment that encourages open discussion and collaboration, enabling learning rather than teaching (Reason and Bradbury 2006). This approach reflects a commitment to flattening hierarchies, valuing the knowledge and perspectives in the room (Chambers 2002; Ledwith and Springett 2022).

Yet, as Box 3.1 illustrates, this is not always straightforward. Creating genuinely inclusive spaces requires moving beyond assumptions about what 'should' work and instead listening carefully to participants' needs and preferences. Our experience shows that what feels welcoming to us as facilitators may feel exclusionary or intimidating to others. Finding this balance can be difficult, and we must remain reflexive about how our identities, professional backgrounds, and expectations inevitably shape the process (Bradbury-Huang 2010).

> **Box 3.1: Embracing different learning needs**
>
> Many people who train as community researchers have not had positive experiences in traditional education. For them, learning needs to feel different – less like a classroom with a teacher at the front and more like a space built around inclusion, flexibility, and respect. As one drug service user put it after a training session: 'I wish school had been like this.'
>
> However, creating inclusive spaces requires careful thought. In one project in York focused on homelessness and access to mental health services, we initially set up a circle of chairs to encourage open discussion. Instead, participants found the layout intimidating as it evoked therapy or Alcoholics Anonymous (AA) meetings. We quickly moved to a nearby café, where conversation flowed freely.
>
> Similarly, in a project with neurodiverse young people in Hackney, large, noisy group sessions hindered participation. By offering a quiet space and ensuring that no one would be put on the spot, one young man not only felt comfortable attending but also went on to take a lead role in analysing data and writing the report. Without these adjustments, he might not have returned.
>
> These experiences underline a core principle of PAR: inclusion depends on listening, observing, and adapting. Moving beyond assumptions about what participants 'should' want – whether noise, energy, or silence – opens the door to richer contributions and ensures that participants can fully engage.

By remaining present but unobtrusive, we support the people we work with to fully immerse themselves in the research process, sharing their unique perspectives and experiences without feeling overshadowed or directed. This ethos extends throughout the entire PAR process, from training sessions to fieldwork and analysis. By prioritising facilitation skills over didactic teaching methods, we strive to promote a more inclusive approach. In our experience, this not only leads to richer insights but also encourages continuous adaptation and refinement of our methods.

From top-down to bottom-up

Our approach is rooted in questioning the status quo and recognising the disparities that often silence or devalue certain groups (Freire 2017; Ledwith and Springett 2022). In our projects, we try to create spaces where different forms of knowledge and expertise – including those that are too often ignored because of class, ethnicity, disability, gender, or other markers of inequality – can be heard and engaged with on equal terms.

We know we cannot eliminate hierarchies or power structures altogether, and PAR is never a perfect process. But it does offer ways of working that make these dynamics more visible and negotiable. Rather than claiming to 'give voice', we see our role as working *with* communities to ensure their perspectives, knowledge, and agency are recognised in the research process and outcomes.

A key part of this work is reflexivity, which means critically reflecting on how our own identities, agendas, and positionalities shape the research process. As feminist and critical scholars have argued, knowledge is always situated and partial (Haraway 1988; Rose 1997). Our social positions influence not only how we frame questions, but also how participants perceive us and what knowledge is shared (Rowe 2014). As Box 3.2 explores, reflexivity requires us to be explicit about our assumptions, to interrogate our own privilege and vulnerability, and to recognise the ways we may simultaneously be 'insiders' and 'outsiders' within a project (Herr and Anderson 2005).

Box 3.2: Asking reflexive questions – seeing ourselves in the research

Being reflexive in PAR means asking hard questions about ourselves and the impact we have on the process. It's not just about *what* we do, but *who* we are and how that shapes the research. Some questions we might ask include the following:

- What lens do I bring?
- What is my agenda?
- What do I already know, and how?
- What do I want to find out?
- What impact do I have on the people who take part?
- In what ways am I an insider? In what ways am I an outsider?

In one project on maternity care, one of the authors trained a group of women who had recently been through the system. At the time, she was visibly pregnant herself. Some of the community researchers worried that listening to difficult birth stories might be hard for her. She explained that this was her second pregnancy and that she too had experienced a traumatic birth the first time round. In that sense, she had 'skin in the game'.

But she was also a white, middle-class woman. She could not fully understand the experiences of the Black African women on the research team, who described the racism, stereotyping, and poor care they had endured. Listening to them opened her eyes to realities she had never faced.

She realised that she was both an 'insider' and an 'outsider' in this project – connected by shared experience of birth trauma, yet distanced by privilege and race. Reflexivity meant recognising both positions, and being honest about how they shaped the research process and her relationships with the team.

Finally, it is important to recognise that a PAR project cannot achieve meaningful change without the active involvement and support of those who hold structural power, including funders, service providers, and other key organisations with resources. As the example in Box 3.3 shows, engagement is critical not only for translating recommendations into practical actions but also for ensuring that the community's knowledge and insights are taken seriously. Without their cooperation, even the most carefully facilitated and reflexive projects risk limited impact or being sidelined once the research ends.

> **Box 3.3: Safeguarding Camden**
>
> Camden Council was concerned that families and young people were not sufficiently informed about safeguarding in the borough and wanted to understand how it was perceived in the community. Members of the Parent Council and users of young people's services took part in PAR training and then engaged with others across Camden to explore awareness, understanding, and barriers.
>
> The research revealed that many people did not know what 'safeguarding' meant and were far more familiar with the previously used term 'child protection'. Other barriers included professional attitudes, fear of being accused of mistreating children, and, for some young people, negative experiences with the very professionals meant to keep them safe.
>
> The participants felt genuinely empowered by the project. Camden Council supported this by arranging meetings between the community researchers and heads of services, giving researchers the opportunity to influence decision makers directly. A particularly memorable moment was when a young man with cerebral palsy described to the Chief of Police an incident where he had been threatened with arrest for being out after dark without a carer. The Head of Children's Services responded warmly to parents

sharing their findings, thanking them and giving each a hug. Creative tools also allowed participants with writing challenges to fully contribute.

The Parent Council went on to deliver their own PAR projects on issues they had identified, and several parents completed a 'Train the Trainer' course, enabling them to upskill others and embed PAR practice within their communities.

From extracting to empowering

Traditional research has made vital contributions to knowledge and practice, and methods such as surveys, interviews, and focus groups remain important tools. Yet in many cases, participants are positioned mainly as providers of information, while researchers retain control over the framing of questions, the analysis of findings, and the dissemination of results (Cornwall and Jewkes 1995).

PAR takes a different approach. Rather than limiting involvement to 'data provision', it engages community researchers at every stage of the process. This can mean shaping the initial research questions, deciding which methods are most appropriate, planning fieldwork, going out and collecting data, analysing what emerges, and co-designing how findings are shared. In doing so, the research is no longer something *done to* people, but something *done with* them.

This way of working is not about rejecting traditional research, but about widening the circle of who gets to define and interpret knowledge (Chambers 1997; Kindon, Pain, and Kesby 2010). By creating opportunities for active participation and shared decision making, PAR can foster a sense of ownership and investment in the process. It also makes findings more relevant, since those most affected by the issues at hand help shape the insights and solutions.

At its best, PAR transforms research from a one-way extraction of information into a collaborative process of empowerment where knowledge is built collectively and mobilised for change (Chambers, 1997, p 154).

From closed to open enquiry

The fourth shift in our approach is to move from closed, structured research designs to more open and exploratory frameworks. Rather than adhering to rigid topic areas or themes, we encourage participants to investigate issues on their own terms within a flexible structure that helps them consider different perspectives.

This openness goes beyond simply asking open-ended questions; it also involves creating an environment that is more creative and liberating, allowing participants to define what is important to them, explore issues holistically, and develop solutions based on their own discoveries (Reason and Bradbury 2006).

At the same time, we recognise that openness can bring discomfort – not only for clients and commissioners, who may prefer the apparent certainty of structured surveys or fixed questions, but also for community researchers and for us as trainers and facilitators. There are moments when the absence of clear boundaries feels unsettling, when we wonder whether we as a team will arrive at the 'right' questions, or whether the process will yield anything meaningful.

Yet this discomfort is part of the practice. PAR requires us to trust the process – to believe that through dialogue, iteration, and reflecting together, the important questions will surface. Our role as practitioners is not to remove the uncertainty, but to hold the space where it can be generative, offering enough structure to prevent drift while leaving room for participants' own insights to emerge. In doing so, we often uncover unexpected findings that matter to community researchers and participants, but which might have been overlooked had the questions been too narrowly defined at the start.

From text-based to visual and verbal approaches

This shift highlights our focus on visual, verbal, and creative methods in PAR, acknowledging that not everyone learns, communicates, or contributes in the same way. Formal interviews or focus groups can feel intimidating or overly 'professional' or academic for some, which may discourage participation. By incorporating visual, creative, and conversational approaches – including diagramming and drawing methods often designed to be accessible to people with varying levels of literacy – we aim to create inclusive spaces that value multiple ways of knowing, exploring, and contributing, and allow people to engage in ways that feel comfortable.

Our practice has drawn inspiration from the work of creative researchers who demonstrate the value of 'arts-based' and visual research methods (Pink 2012; Mannay 2021; Kara 2020). Approaches such as photovoice, participatory video, theatre, storytelling, mapping, and collage allow participants to represent their own experiences in ways that are meaningful to them (Wang and Burris 1997; Mitchell 2011). These methods can challenge dominant narratives, generate powerful new insights, and communicate findings in accessible and emotionally resonant forms.

We have also found that creativity does not end with data collection. Increasingly, we experiment with how findings are shared whether through community exhibitions, performances, or collaborations with musicians and visual artists. This makes the research more impactful and accessible, while also contributing to wider debates about what counts as legitimate research output (Leavy 2015). It's really important for us to share research findings in ways other than written reports or academic papers, so that more people can access and engage with the results.

One of the most rewarding aspects of this work has been collaborating with artists and creatives on equal terms. The cross-pollination of disciplines, made possible by the openness of PAR, has enabled us to draw on diverse perspectives and experiment with new ways of working. By fostering these partnerships, we can harness the unique strengths and expertise of each discipline, leading to more innovative and impactful outcomes. By working with artists from the communities we engage with, we both support their work and gain from their expertise in developing culturally relevant art.

The following reflection (see Box 3.4) from community researcher Callum Perrin illustrates how creative approaches – in this case, music – can transform the way in which research findings are shared and experienced. It shows how participatory methods can move beyond conventional reports and presentations, engaging participants and audiences in more embodied, accessible, and inclusive ways.

> **Box 3.4: Community researcher reflection – sharing findings through song**
>
> Using songs was an unexpected and interesting way to share some of our research conclusions; although I was initially unsure about its potential effectiveness, in practice it turned out to be a genuinely innovative and actually quite subtle method of sharing and embodying PAR outcomes.
>
> As a community participatory action researcher, I was surprised when Rowena asked if I'd be interested in writing some songs using our research findings. She knew I was a singer and composer, but I'd assumed this was outside my remit as a researcher, so it was exciting to be asked to apply some of my other skills to the project. The idea was to work with Rachel, a community music practitioner and choir leader, to share these songs at the closing event at Dulwich Picture Gallery.
>
> For the songs, I used some of the single sentences which we had come up with to summarise different aspects of our research findings, such as 'Don't be afraid of the difficult', 'Let me in', and 'Show me me'. I turned each into a simple round with three melody lines, with the voices harmonising and overlapping at different points. I sent three of these ideas to Rachel, who used her community singing experience to carefully simplify each vocal line, making them easier to sing for people who don't usually sing.
>
> The singing sessions were held in the mausoleum at Dulwich Picture Gallery – the circular shape of the space was perfect for singing in a circle, creating a sense of intimacy and nonhierarchy. Despite this intimacy, the lively acoustics of the space, with its hard surfaces and domed ceiling, also gave a sense of scale and volume during the singing. This helped lower participant's inhibitions, as you could hear less of each individual (and yourself) and more of the overall collective.

Additionally, holding the singing sessions in the mausoleum tied in nicely with what we discovered during our research – in particular, the desire for the community to access certain cultural and physical spaces from which they felt excluded. The mausoleum at Dulwich Picture Gallery is often either closed off entirely, with visitors only able to look inside from behind a barrier; or it is only accessible to visitors who attend the temporary exhibitions, which is more expensive than only visiting the permanent collection. It was exciting to not only access the mausoleum space, but also to linger and actually make some noise, transforming the space and our expectations of it.

Rachel held two singing sessions at different points during the closing event, giving most visitors the opportunity to attend if they were able to. The sessions began with a simple warm up, before moving on to singing the songs themselves, which Rachel gradually increased in complexity, carefully introducing each new vocal line, and splitting the choir up into different sections. Even participants who were clearly unconfident at the beginning of each session were singing loudly by the end.

I was initially unsure whether songs which only contained the repetition of a single sentence could actually communicate anything from our actual research. My fear was that the act of singing would make the words generic, turning them from language into pure sound and stripping them of meaning in the process. However, I hadn't considered both the context of the closing event, and the collective ritual of singing itself. The singing sessions took place after we had presented our research to visitors and had fully contextualised our research, speaking in-depth about the outcomes. Therefore, when singing, participants already understood what the lyrics were referring to and why they mattered. The embodied act of singing together allowed us to process those words collectively – it was a reminder that these research outcomes were the result of an embedded community, collective process, which was only achievable

> through the emphasis of PAR on co-creation and dialogue. Rather than removing the meaning, singing actually added weight and context to both the research outcomes and the research methods used.
>
> Ultimately, I feel like singing was a way of bringing the research full circle – words and reflections which were generated by in-depth community engagement were brought back into an informal community setting through the act of singing. Sharing community research is too often restricted to dry reports and abstract policy recommendations, so it's exciting to use music, embodiment, and fun to make these outcomes more accessible and relevant to communities it's meant to serve.
>
> *Calum Perrin, Community Researcher, Dulwich Picture Gallery*

Ultimately, this approach reinforces the idea that knowledge is not siloed within any one field or method, but enriched through the exchange of ideas across disciplines. Visual and creative methods are not an 'add-on' to participatory research, but are central to making it more inclusive, equitable, and transformative.

From individual to group perspectives

This final coupling emphasises our focus on both individual and group perspectives in PAR, recognising that people may feel more comfortable contributing in different ways and contexts. While we value individual stories and viewpoints, our work often centres on understanding group or community perspectives (Chambers 1997; Reason and Bradbury 2006). This approach encourages participants to learn from each other and challenge their assumptions. Emphasising group perspectives also reinforces our commitment to go beyond simple data collection, prioritising relationship building, knowledge sharing, and moving to action together.

However, it is important to note that communities are not monolithic or homogeneous. Within any community or researcher team, there will be multiple subgroups, perspectives, and power dynamics (Kindon, Pain, and Kesby 2010). Paying attention to these dynamics can be challenging: friction may arise within community researcher teams, or participants may encounter viewpoints during fieldwork with which they do not agree. Negotiating these differences requires careful facilitation, active listening, and explicit attention to respect and inclusivity. In practice, this often involves structured discussions, small breakouts, or paired work to ensure that quieter voices are heard and dominant voices are moderated. Techniques such as role playing, scenario planning, and reflective journaling help participants build understanding and empathy for different points of view.

Behaviours and attitudes

The transformative shifts outlined earlier are complemented by a set of behaviours and attitudes that guide our practice. Whereas the shifts describe the structural and methodological changes that underpin our participatory approach, these behaviours and attitudes highlight the *how* of working alongside communities. As Chambers (2002) emphasises, participatory practice depends not only on methods but also on the conduct, humility, and attitudes of the researcher. We have adapted his list of participatory behaviours, and attitudes into our own framework, which we explore with community researchers as part of their training and reflective practice. They include the following:

1. **Show respect:** Acknowledge and value the diverse perspectives, experiences, and knowledge of community members.
2. **Establish rapport:** Build connections and develop trust through open communication and active listening.
3. **Abandon preconceptions and maintain neutrality:** Set aside personal biases and assumptions, allowing community members to guide the research process.
4. **Hand over the stick (power):** Empower community members by giving them a leading role in decision making and knowledge production.
5. **Watch, listen, and learn:** Be attentive to community dynamics and practices, recognising that you are a learner as well as a researcher.

6. **Be self-critical and self-aware:** Reflect on your own positionality and the potential impact of your presence on the research process.
7. **Be flexible:** Adapt to the unique needs, preferences, and circumstances of the community, ensuring that the research process is responsive and inclusive.
8. **Support and share:** Provide resources, knowledge, and skills to help community members engage in the research process and take action based on the findings.
9. **Be honest:** Maintain transparency about the research purpose, process, and potential outcomes, fostering trust and accountability.
10. **Embrace error:** Recognise that mistakes and missteps are opportunities for learning and growth, both for yourself and the community.
11. **They can do it:** Have confidence in community members' ability to drive change and contribute valuable insights throughout the research process.

We actively try to uphold these behaviours and attitudes in every project. Happily, 'be honest' and 'embrace error' are embedded in the framework, reminding us that it is okay not to get everything right. As Box 3.5 illustrates, it is not always easy or possible to get these right.

> **Box 3.5: Navigating strong opinions**
>
> It can be very difficult for community members who have deep knowledge and 'skin in the game' to put aside their own points of view when their opinions are strong. In one project in South Tyneside, we worked with a team of community researchers on a community action plan to improve local housing estates. At times, researchers would finish interviewees' sentences or answer for them, despite our guidance. We had to revisit the classroom to reflect on this behaviour. Most of the team understood and adjusted, but one longstanding, highly influential community

> member struggled to hold herself back and refrain from commenting, highlighting the challenges of balancing expertise with participatory principles.

In this section, we outlined the ethos that underlies our approach to PAR and what sets us apart from more traditional research methodologies. Our commitment to a series of transformative shifts, including balancing individual and collective perspectives, fostering trust, and maintaining an adaptive approach, pushes us to try and create a collaborative and empowering research environment. Alongside these shifts, we emphasise the importance of a set of behaviours and attitudes that uphold equity, respect, and collaboration as core values in our research practice.

The Participatory Action Research process

This section sets out our refined PAR process, which has been developed over many years, to ensure that our PAR projects are not only manageable and achievable but also transparent and aligned with our ethos. Understanding and adhering to a well-defined process is fundamental to effective project management. From a transparency perspective, it is crucial that all stakeholders are clear about each stage of the research process and its impacts, enabling us to practise what we preach in terms of our PAR values.

In order to clearly outline our approach, we have developed a process diagram (see Figure 3.1) that draws inspiration from Kurt Lewin's reflective cycle of action research. Lewin's model progresses from research (understanding) to action (change) to evaluation (learning) and back to research. In our adaptation, we include two additional high-level phases specific to our projects, which involve peer and community researchers as core components, adapted from Vaughn and Jacque (2020) and Zuber-Skerrit (1996).

The remainder of this chapter explores each stage of our adapted PAR process step by step. For every stage, we draw on our experience of working with community researchers to highlight the distinctive features, common challenges, and practical strategies that shape our approach.

Figure 3.1: Stages of our Participatory Action Research process

Partnering
- Collaborate with commissioners and clients
- Recruit community researcher team

Preparation
- Train the community researcher team
- Establish collective ground rules and ways of working together
- Introduce and practice research tools and techniques

Research
- Design the research together
- First phase of fieldwork
- Facilitate mid-way analysis and reflection sessions
- Second phase of research
- Final analysis sessions

Action
- Identify possible actions
- Share research findings and gather feedback from stakeholders
- Develop an action plan
- Develop final report and other outputs

Evaluation
- Measure the impact of changes
- Assess emerging issues and challenges

Repeat the cycle as needed
- Feed learning back into the process
- Begin a new cycle where appropriate

Partnering: establishing collaborations

As independent practitioners, the origins of our PAR projects are diverse, encompassing various partnerships and funding sources. We collaborate with numerous organisations across sectors, including public sector entities, health authorities, professional bodies, cultural institutions, charities, and community-based organisations. These partnerships may arise from direct commissions, tender processes, joint funding proposals, or promoting PAR benefits to existing and new clients.

While partnerships can be fruitful, they may also face challenges. Difficulties often stem from misunderstandings, assumptions, or institutional biases that perceive PAR as less rigorous or scientific than other methodologies. Despite progress in addressing these misconceptions, such as establishing quality standards for PAR projects and emphasising the rigour and quality assurance inherent in the practice, more work is needed to promote widespread acceptance (Rowley, Doyle, and Hay 2013) (Young Foundation 2024).

Our experience highlights the importance of transparency, open communication, and a clear understanding of roles and expectations in fostering successful partnerships. By addressing potential obstacles and advocating for the value of PAR, we aim to encourage organisations to embrace this collaborative and transformative approach to research.

Checklist for vetting Participatory Action Research projects and partnerships

To ensure the success and impact of our PAR projects, we have developed a checklist to assess potential partnerships and projects (see Figure 3.2). This checklist helps identify key factors that may hinder the effectiveness of a PAR project, such as time constraints, limited budgets, or lack of partner commitment. By using this checklist, we aim to maintain the quality, equitability, and impact of our research.

Collaborative brief development

Once all partners are aligned, a contract is in place, and the checklist criteria are met, we initiate a collaborative briefing

Figure 3.2: Checklist for assessing Participatory Action Research partnerships

process to establish a shared understanding of the project's scope and aims. Key aspects of this process include the following:

1. **Encouraging open-ended questions:** Guiding clients to pose broad questions, allowing room for exploration and the potential for unexpected discoveries. This approach empowers community researchers to shape specific questions, methods, and fieldwork strategies.
2. **Setting project constraints:** Identifying boundaries such as topic areas, geographical communities, or demographic groups to maintain a manageable focus while still allowing flexibility.
3. **Clarifying roles and responsibilities:** Outlining each partner's contributions and expectations, ensuring that all parties understand their unique roles in the PAR process.
4. **Creating a project timeline:** Developing a shared timeline, including milestones, to guide progress and keep all parties informed.

5. **Stakeholder mapping:** Identifying and engaging relevant stakeholders who should be involved or informed about the project, ensuring broad community representation.
6. **Leveraging past experiences:** Reviewing previous projects to identify best practices, potential challenges, and lessons learned.
7. **Addressing concerns and challenges:** Discussing potential obstacles and collaboratively developing strategies to address them.

By collaboratively developing a strong project brief and fostering a supportive foundation based on trust, we set the stage for successful PAR projects. This collaborative foundation also supports the next stage: recruiting community researchers in partnership with the commissioning organisation, ensuring that the team reflects both community needs and project goals. The 'magic' of PAR expressed in Box 3.6 can only be fully realised when investment is made in building good working relationships with commissioners in the early stages of a project.

> **Box 3.6: Commissioners' reflections – the magic of Participatory Action Research**
>
> I think there's something special, almost magical in the PAR process. Working alongside the people who are directly affected by decisions and enabling them to contribute honestly towards their future is an honour!
>
> *Susie Crome, Commissioner, Tower Hamlets Public Health*

Recruiting the community researcher team

Following brief development, our next focus is on recruiting a community researcher team that brings the necessary skills, aptitudes, and experiences to the PAR project. Working closely with our clients and commissioners, we identify the specific attributes needed for each project, which may include experience with a particular issue, membership in a specific community of interest, or connection to a geographical community.

The community researcher team plays a vital role in facilitating access to a broader network of participants in our PAR projects. Ensuring that the team members have lived experience of the issue under study is crucial, as they bring invaluable expertise and understanding of the topic, as well as connections to others impacted by the issue.

In our experience, the recruitment process is most successful when our client or commissioning organisations have strong connections within the local community or access to frontline staff and community champions. Building on existing partnerships with trusted community-based organisations can greatly enhance the recruitment process, as these partners often recognise the value of community researcher opportunities and are eager to share them with their beneficiaries.

Community members are more likely to learn about and feel encouraged to apply for community researcher roles when they hear about the opportunities through trusted individuals or organisations. While this is not always possible, we often employ a combination of approaches, including word-of-mouth, social media outreach, and placing posters and leaflets in relevant community venues within our target areas. In reality, recruitment often hits snags and setbacks, as Box 3.7 illustrates, recruitment may require adaptability, persistence, and local knowledge to reach the people you want to engage. As Box 3.8 shows, recruitment mediated by gatekeepers can create selection bias and limit the diversity of perspectives in your community researcher team.

> **Box 3.7: Flexible, on-the-ground recruitment**
>
> In a project for a heritage organisation in a rural part of southern England, initial attempts to recruit community researchers via social media and community partners were largely unsuccessful. To reach the intended communities, the client team adopted a more hands-on approach: walking the streets and posting opportunities on community noticeboards and in public venues across rural and coastal areas. This flexible, on-the-ground approach eventually led to the recruitment of a diverse community researcher team.

> **Box 3.8: Recruitment controlled by gatekeepers**
>
> In a recent peer research project focusing on young people's health needs, the local youth work service was asked by the local authority to help recruit participants. The youth service approached local schools, resulting in a group composed mainly of high achievers and school council members. While capable, this group was not representative of the broader population of young people in the area.

Regardless of the recruitment strategies employed, it is vital to develop a clear set of information sheets that provide prospective community researchers with essential details about the opportunity. These materials should outline the scope of the work, the responsibilities involved, and the benefits of participation. By providing this information upfront, we ensure that potential community researchers have a thorough understanding of the role and can make an informed decision about whether to apply.

To further enhance our recruitment efforts and promote diversity within our community researcher teams, we have recently adopted the Positive Action Recruitment Roadmap (British Museum 2020). While originally developed for the museum world, this roadmap provides valuable guidance and practical tools that can be applied across various sectors.

The Positive Action Recruitment Roadmap encourages engaging a more diverse range of individuals through partnership building, taster days, and interviews. By incorporating these strategies into our recruitment process, we aim to create a more inclusive environment that attracts candidates from a wide range of backgrounds, experiences, and perspectives. One of the key strengths of the Positive Action Recruitment Roadmap is its emphasis on skills and competencies rather than traditional qualifications and experience. By prioritising these factors, we can identify candidates who possess the necessary abilities to contribute effectively to our projects, regardless of their formal educational background or work history.

When recruiting community researchers for PAR projects, there are several skills and competencies that are particularly valuable, such as the following:

1. **Enthusiasm and genuine interest in the topic area:** Passionate individuals who are invested in the subject matter are more likely to be engaged and committed throughout the research process.
2. **Local knowledge and connections:** Community researchers with a deep understanding of the local area and its residents can provide valuable insights and help identify relevant participants for the project.
3. **Active listening skills:** The ability to listen attentively and engage meaningfully with others is crucial for building trust and facilitating productive conversations during the research process.
4. **Communication skills:** Community researchers should be able to communicate effectively with participants, team members, and other stakeholders.
5. **Questioning nature:** Curiosity and the ability to ask thoughtful, probing questions are essential for uncovering new insights and driving the research forward.
6. **Respecting difference:** maintaining an open-minded approach, respecting different viewpoints, and being sensitive to the needs of different groups.

Pay and terms: ensuring fair compensation and support

An essential aspect of recruiting and engaging community researchers in PAR projects is addressing the critical issue of pay and terms. In recent years, there has been a growing awareness of the need to fairly compensate people for their valuable contributions to research, particularly when working with clients and commissioners who have the resources and power to provide financial support (NIHR, 2024).

While it may be appropriate for some projects, particularly those that originate from the voluntary sector or are bottom-up commissioned, in order to involve community researchers on a voluntary basis with the provision of training and support, it is no longer acceptable to expect people to undertake this important work without compensation when working with relatively well-resourced organisations that employ professional staff members on reasonable salaries.

As a general guideline, we strive to pay community researchers the living wage in the specific area where we are conducting the PAR project. This approach helps ensure that compensation is fair and aligned with local economic realities.

However, it is essential to acknowledge that the nature of community researcher projects often entails limited duration and part-time work. This raises important considerations regarding the feasibility and sustainability of providing a living wage for positions that may not offer full-time hours or long-term employment.

Given that community researchers are typically hired as freelancers, it is crucial to provide support and guidance regarding their tax and self-assessment responsibilities. Many individuals may be unfamiliar with the intricacies of freelance work, and it is essential to ensure they have the necessary information and resources to navigate these processes effectively.

The complexity of payment further increases when community researchers are receiving benefits, as we must ensure that their compensation as community researchers does not negatively affect their benefit entitlements.

To mitigate potential impacts on benefit entitlements, we may consider structuring payment terms that spread compensation across a longer period, thereby minimising the risk of exceeding income thresholds that could jeopardise their eligibility for benefits.

Additionally, we recognise the importance of providing community researchers with access to organisations that specialise in offering assistance with benefits-related matters. By connecting community researchers with these resources, we can help them navigate the intricacies of the benefits system and make informed decisions regarding their participation in PAR projects.

Useful guidance on payment for research participants includes the following:

1. The UK Research and Innovation published a document entitled 'Guidance on Payment for Public Partners',

which provides recommendations and considerations for compensating participants, including ethical and legal aspects (UKRI 2024).
2. The Social Research Association has a set of 'Ethical guidelines' that address payment and incentives for research participants, discussing fairness, proportionality, and potential unintended consequences (SRA 2021).
3. The Economic and Social Research Council's 'Framework for research ethics' includes a section on payments to research participants, addressing issues such as coercion, reimbursement of expenses, and implications for benefits (ESRC 2022).

These resources provide valuable insights into best practices for compensating research participants while navigating the complexities of benefits and other ethical implications.

Fostering career opportunities and legacy beyond individual projects

Beyond the immediate scope of individual PAR projects, we are committed to creating lasting impact and opening doors to broader career opportunities for community researchers. We work closely with our clients and commissioners to identify potential pathways for community researchers to secure further work within their organisations. This collaborative approach not only benefits community researchers by helping them gain a foothold in sectors that can be challenging to access, such as the arts and heritage industries, but also enriches these fields by introducing diverse perspectives and expertise.

Additionally, we recognise that the experience gained through PAR projects often leads to work opportunities beyond our direct client sector. We support community researchers in pursuing these prospects by providing references, guidance, and ongoing encouragement.

Furthermore, we strive to create additional opportunities for community researchers to engage in future projects, prioritising higher compensation rates for those who have completed a project and undergone PAR training. This may involve inviting experienced community researchers to participate in training sessions for professionals and academics interested in PAR, as well as engaging them in subsequent projects where their skills and local knowledge align with the research objectives.

Reflections in Box 3.9, shared by Larysa Agbaso, illustrate how involvement in PAR can equip community researchers with skills, confidence, and professional credibility that extend far beyond the life of a single project.

> **Box 3.9: Community researcher reflections – discovering a treasure box of tools**
>
> Being a community researcher was like discovering a treasure box. At that time, I was part of a so-called marginalised community, voiceless, living with personal trauma, loss of identity, and a sense of injustice. It was hard to trust. I was nothing.
>
> This treasure box contained a lot of valuable things. Among the things in that treasure box were respect, validation, recognition, support, inspiration, self-worth, trust, knowledge, and skills. The first step was meeting like-minded people with similar experiences, which created safety and began to build trust. We learnt a lot. We learnt from the trainers. We learnt from each other. We learnt through sharing what we knew. For me, it was essential that research was approached in a trauma-informed way. My voice was heard. My knowledge was valued. Participants were treated with dignity. My lived experience of displacement and my expertise as a trauma-informed teacher helped me recognise unspoken needs, create safety, and ensure that every stage of the research centred participants' agency and wellbeing.
>
> Years later, those treasures have not lost their value. The participatory research tools and skills I gained remain gold. I still use them in my teaching, my advocacy work, and even my personal planning. This experience set me on the research path and shaped my vision of what research can be when power is shared and sensitivity and ethics guide every step.
>
> *Larysa Agbaso, Community Researcher, from British Red Cross PAR project*

While individual projects can be empowering, more needs to be done to establish structured career pathways for community researchers. This requires institutional support, including mechanisms to provide ongoing training, recognition, and progression opportunities, so that the skills gained through PAR projects are not lost once a project concludes. Examples from further afield provide inspiration. In the US, doctoral programs such as the PhD in Community Research and Action at Vanderbilt University's Peabody College equip students with the skills and knowledge necessary to pursue careers in community-focused research, policy, and advocacy (Vanderbilt University n.d.). Developing similar pathways in the UK could help create sustainable opportunities for community researchers seeking to carry on in their research careers.

Preparation: the training

In the preparation phase of our PAR process, we focus on investing in community researchers, helping them build the confidence, skills, and knowledge needed to plan and undertake their fieldwork effectively.

Our training typically spans five days, prioritising hands-on learning and practical experience. We follow the '20% learning from the front, 80% learning through doing' principle. This approach ensures that participants not only acquire essential skills but also experience the facilitation and participatory techniques they are expected to use in the field.

Key components of our training include the following:

1. **Practical exercises:** Design training activities that allow participants to actively engage in the skills and methods they will use during their projects, promoting experiential learning and retention. These include participatory techniques which will be covered in this chapter, as well as the specific visual, creative, and diagramming tools used to structure, guide, and capture conversations during fieldwork, which are covered in Chapter 4.
2. **Leading by example:** Facilitate the training sessions in a way that mirrors the desired behaviours and techniques participants should use in their own research, creating a cohesive and consistent learning environment.

3. **Encouraging reflection:** Integrate opportunities for participants to reflect on their learning experiences, enabling them to assess their progress, identify areas for improvement, and deepen their understanding of PAR methodologies.

Participatory from the start

Our approach to fostering a participatory environment right from the beginning is heavily influenced by the work of Robert Chambers. Chambers emphasises the importance of creating an inclusive atmosphere where everyone feels valued and can contribute their unique perspectives. As he notes: 'Participation is a mindset, a way of thinking about and behaving in relationships, not just a set of techniques' (2002, p 11).

Priya Parker's *The Art of Gathering* (2018) adds another important layer: participation begins with the purpose and design of the gathering itself. Parker highlights that meetings and workshops often default to habit rather than being intentionally designed to serve their participants. She calls for facilitators to be deliberate about setting the tone, establishing shared purpose, and breaking down hierarchical barriers so that everyone feels that their presence matters.

We recognise that people may feel nervous when entering our training space, so we prioritise putting them at ease and minimising the perceived distance between us as trainers and them as participants. We aim to create an environment that acknowledges our different roles, yet fosters a sense of shared learning and collaboration:

1. **Pre-workshop introductions:** To ensure participants have a familiar face during the workshop, we arrange for them to meet at least one of us before the training session.
2. **Addressing access needs:** We inquire about participants' access requirements prior to the workshop to ensure that the space and materials are accessible for everyone.
3. **Community-based venues:** Choosing non-corporate, neutral venues within the community helps to create a more welcoming atmosphere. We seek feedback on the venue and make changes as needed.
4. **Involving participants in setup:** By assigning small roles at the beginning of the workshop, such as setting up flipcharts

or arranging tables, we encourage a sense of ownership and belonging among participants.

Icebreakers

Recognising the importance of creating a welcoming and inclusive environment from the start, we have compiled a collection of icebreakers that we use in our training workshops (West 1999). These activities are designed to transcend professional hierarchies, promote interaction, and create a level playing field for all participants:

1. **Seed Mixer:** Participants swap seed varieties with one another until they have one of each type, fostering movement and conversation.
2. **Bead Stringing:** Participants exchange beads and string them together, creating a tactile and low-stress experience that encourages connection.
3. **Key Moments:** Participants share the stories and meanings behind the keys they carry, fostering self-reflection, personal storytelling, and building connections.
4. **Smile Sharing:** Participants share something that made them smile recently, revealing their humanity and encouraging lighthearted conversation.
5. **Zip! Zap! Pow!:** participants form a circle and quickly pass 'energy' to the right by saying 'zip', to the left by saying 'zap', or to anyone in the circle by saying 'pow!' with accompanying hand gestures; the game speeds up as it progresses, and the goal is to be the last person remaining who successfully catches and passes the 'energy'.

Box 3.10 shows how a gentle icebreaker can make people feel at ease and allow people to have some fun.

> **Box 3.10: The power of icebreakers that generate laughter**
>
> When used thoughtfully, icebreaker games can create a fun and welcoming atmosphere for training sessions. They

> provide an opportunity for participants to take a break from their daily challenges and connect with others in a lighthearted way. A community researcher shared her experience after suffering a bereavement: 'Taking part in an icebreaker [Zip! Zap! Pow!] in the training course made me laugh for the first time in many years.'

These icebreakers serve as valuable tools for breaking down barriers, creating a comfortable atmosphere, and nurturing a sense of connection among participants.

For those seeking additional icebreaker activities and facilitation techniques, there are numerous resources available. Here are a few suggestions:

- Augusto Boal's *Games for Actors and Non-actors* (2002), which offers participatory theatre games and warm-ups.
- Michael Michalko's *Thinkertoys: A Handbook of Creative-Thinking Techniques* (2006), which provides structured yet playful exercises to spark imagination and problem solving.
- Sarah Stein Greenberg's *Creative Acts for Curious People* (2021), a collection of creative activities that help groups tackle problems creatively and collaboratively.
- Liberating Structures (https://www.liberatingstructures.com/), which provide adaptable methods for participatory group work.

Participant-driven ground rules and the 'Bike Rack' technique

To foster a participatory atmosphere in our training sessions, we incorporate a variety of techniques that serve as the foundation for collaborative teamwork. While establishing ground rules is a widely used method, we recognise that this process can occasionally feel repetitive. To maintain engagement and encourage a bit of rebelliousness, we have introduced alternative approaches such as the 'Ingredients for Terrible Teams' exercise. In this activity we invite participants to brainstorm and list behaviours that lead to ineffective collaboration. By identifying the traits of poor teamwork, the group becomes more aware of the importance of positive, participatory behaviours.

This exercise also injects humour into the session, creating a lighthearted atmosphere that enhances engagement. By inviting the team to reflect on their expectations of one another and of the facilitators, we seek to promote a more democratic and tailored approach.

To maintain focus during discussions and prevent tangents from derailing the conversation, we implement the 'Bike Rack' technique. This method allows participants to 'park' their ideas, thoughts, or questions that may not be immediately relevant to the current topic. By creating a designated space for these points, the group can continue with the primary discussion while ensuring that no valuable insights are lost.

While the 'Bike Rack' technique may not be heavily utilised in every training session, we encourage its use to promote efficient and streamlined discussions. This approach offers the following benefits:

1. **Prevents tangents:** By providing a place to store unrelated ideas, participants are less likely to divert the conversation away from the main topic.
2. **Preserves insights:** The 'Bike Rack' serves as a repository for potentially valuable ideas or questions that may not fit within the current discussion, but could be revisited later.
3. **Encourages self-regulation:** Participants are empowered to manage their own contributions to the conversation, fostering a sense of responsibility and ownership within the group.

Client or commissioner briefing

An essential component of our training sessions is the briefing, which provides a valuable opportunity for clients to share their vision, goals, and expectations. To make this process more engaging and interactive, we often transform the traditional presentation format into a dynamic experience, such as a tour or an interactive discussion.

Key aspects of an interactive briefing include the following:

1. **Client-led tour:** Clients guide participants through their facilities or relevant locations, providing an immersive

experience that deepens understanding. Even better, community researchers take clients on their own tour, highlighting people and places that are significant to them.
2. **Concise presentation or talk:** Clients deliver a short, to-the-point presentation that emphasises the importance of the project, clarifies its objectives, and highlights the desired impact. This will ensure participants have a clear understanding of the PAR project's significance and goals.
3. **Open dialogue:** Clients engage in conversation with participants, answering questions and fostering a collaborative atmosphere from the outset.

The interactive briefing serves a crucial role in our training sessions, providing participants with an opportunity to connect with the client on a more personal level. Through this process, we encourage clients to welcome community researchers as valuable members of their team, promoting a sense of belonging and support within the organisation. Key objectives of the interactive briefing include the following:

1. **Building rapport:** By engaging with clients in an informal and dynamic setting, participants feel more comfortable approaching them with questions or concerns throughout the research process.
2. **Clarifying research objectives:** Through open dialogue, clients can communicate their vision and specific research questions, ensuring that all participants have a shared understanding of the project's goals and scope. At this point, we set up a specific tool to capture questions called the 'Questions Bank', which are refined and iterated by the community researchers over the course of the fieldwork.
3. **Exploring potential impact:** The interactive briefing allows participants to ask questions about the potential impact of the research, fostering critical thinking and setting realistic expectations for the project's outcomes.

Ultimately, the interactive briefing serves as a vital step in aligning the goals and expectations of both the client and the community researchers.

Starting the research from day 1

One of the unique aspects of our approach is that we initiate the research process from the very first day of training, exploring the lived experiences of our community researchers. As we practise tools and techniques, their opinions and insights are not only considered valid but also play an integral role in shaping the research direction.

Incorporating this approach offers several benefits:

1. **Boosting morale:** Starting the research from day 1 creates a sense of accomplishment and motivation, as participants feel they are making immediate progress towards their goals.
2. **Sharing perspectives:** Community researchers have the opportunity to share their own thoughts, experiences, and ideas, contributing to a richer understanding of the topic under study.
3. **Documenting and parking ideas and experiences:** By documenting their initial thoughts and reflections during training, participants can 'park' these ideas and approach field research with open ears and, as far as possible, an unbiased mindset, allowing them to focus on gathering diverse perspectives and insights from others.

Team roles

Community research projects are undeniably a collaborative effort, with each team member playing a critical role in ensuring the success and effectiveness of the research. When conducting fieldwork, it is essential to have at least three individuals involved, each fulfilling one of the following distinct roles:

1. **The Facilitator:** Leads the community through the PAR tool, asking thought-provoking questions and encouraging in-depth discussions to gather valuable insights and perspectives.
2. **The Observer:** Takes a broad view of the research session, documenting essential aspects such as discussions, behaviours, conditions, participant engagement levels, and other

noteworthy observations not captured by the tool itself. The observer also records details about the session's date, time, location, and demographics of participants.
3. **The Anti-saboteur:** Identifies and addresses potential hindrances to participant engagement, such as dominating personalities or external distractions, to ensure an inclusive and balanced discussion (Jones 1995).

During our training sessions, we delve into each of these roles, with a particular focus on honing facilitation skills. Exercises include using a 'Body Map' (see Chapter 4 for more on these) to draw out participant traits, a role-play activity to distinguish between open and closed questions, and an ideation exercise to identify key ingredients of active listening. These exercises provide participants with a solid foundation in each role, allowing them to adapt and collaborate effectively throughout their PAR projects.

Ultimately it is the hands-on experience of trying out the visual tools, diagramming and creative methods (which are set out in Chapter 4) that is crucial for building confidence and proficiency in building facilitation skills. The bulk of our training course is focused on them, with participants taking turns facilitating visual tools with their fellow community researchers. This approach provides a safe, supportive environment for individuals to hone their facilitation skills, gain constructive feedback, and learn from each other's experiences.

Engaging and effective workshop design techniques

To ensure our research activities are both productive and engaging, we employ a variety of workshop design techniques that foster individual reflection, collaboration, and dynamic group work. These techniques include the following:

1. **Individual reflection:** Participants are encouraged to reflect on their own experiences, ideas, and insights before sharing with pairs and then the whole group.
2. **Listing and clustering:** Ideas and thoughts are captured on Post-it notes, which are then grouped and clustered to

identify common themes and connections (Chambers 2002, pp 134–135).
3. **Carousel:** Teams work on a specific tool and rotate to other teams, sharing knowledge and insights while learning from one another (Walker 2020).
4. **Teaching and learning cycles:** Each group works on a tool, with one member staying behind to teach the next group about the tool and its facilitation (Chambers 2002, p 149).
5. **Gallery walls:** Completed tools are displayed on walls, allowing for quick feedback and idea sharing within a short timeframe, typically two minutes.

By incorporating these diverse workshop design techniques, we create an interactive and collaborative environment that stimulates creativity and encourages participation.

Another essential aspect of our workshop design, which comes with experience and is harder to pin down, is being agile in our approaches. While we always have a plan, we've learned to adapt it as needed based on the group's dynamics and needs. Over time, we've become better at leaving more space for activities, avoiding the tendency to cram too much content, and ensuring participants feel energised rather than exhausted.

Sometimes, we find it necessary to adjust timings, remove or add activities, or re-arrange the order of events. This adaptability requires attentive observation, active listening, and the ability to read the energy in the room. We pay close attention to participants' needs, remain open to feedback, and embrace spontaneity when it occurs. Evaluation tools such as Evaluation Betty and the Pizza Pie (explored further in Chapter 4) help us reflect on what is working in real time and adapt accordingly.

Research design, fieldwork support and analysis

This section sets out how community researchers are supported in planning and carrying out their research. These include using participatory tools to build on the community expertise in the room to identify key issues or questions and develop a fieldwork plan; the support provided during fieldwork; practical aspects such as gathering data and recording demographics; and the sequencing of the tools from broad to narrow discussions, and from gathering ideas to defining and agreeing a set of actions.

Designing the research

Alongside the Question Bank (introduced earlier), we also work with community researchers to collaboratively review the tools available (discussed in Chapter 4) and identify which are most relevant to the project. From this discussion, we co-create a *fieldwork guide* – a practical document that outlines the research's primary purpose, key questions, and a tailored selection of tools. The guide is intended to provide structure and support while still encouraging researchers to adapt, experiment, and respond to the dynamics of their fieldwork.[1]

After finalising the fieldwork guide, we dedicate time to planning when and where the research will take place, drawing on the community researchers' local knowledge and insights. We use participatory tools such as mapping and timeline creation (covered in Chapter 4) to identify potential locations and participant groups, and to shape an overall research schedule.

At first, trainers accompany community researchers in supported fieldwork sessions to build confidence and familiarity with the tools and techniques. From there, researchers are encouraged to draw on their own networks, priorities, and ideas for subsequent fieldwork. We continue to provide logistical support where needed while creating space for researchers to take the lead. As Box 3.11 illustrates, this approach is crucial because community researchers are often best placed to identify the right people to engage, drawing on their deep local knowledge and commitment to their community.

> **Box 3.11: Community researcher reflections – local knowledge in action**
>
> The rural community is a very special one in which to grow up. Despite changing trends, the onset of technology,

> and the climate challenges we all face, there are still very deeply embedded opinions and practices relating to the care of our countryside and the livelihoods that depend on it. Our countryside towns, parks, footpaths, and country houses are there for us all to enjoy, and ensuring that this remains the case is a steadily growing challenge for those who devote their working and often family life to its care. I consider it a privilege to be a part of this community, one that has been part of my family life for as long as I can remember, and one that is still rooted in hard work and integrity. Working as a researcher with the Pet Detectives gave me the opportunity to get to the heart of what really matters to those in the rural community I share and visitors to our area alike. The community research tools we were trained to use uncovered many different opinions and perspectives from all our contributors, leading to a very in-depth report.
>
> *Sarah Tate, Community Researcher, Petworth Detectives*

Fieldwork itself takes many shapes and unfolds in a wide range of everyday community settings. Sessions have taken place at bus stops, in hairdressers and nail salons, local pubs, children's play parks, schools, parent-and-baby groups, student unions, agricultural fairs, Scouts and Guides groups, art galleries, care homes, corner shops, community cafés, bingo sessions, farmers' markets, and even in people's own frontyards. Conversations have been held with younger and older people, with people of many ethnicities, in community languages, in small groups, and one-to-one. This diversity of setting and format not only makes the research more inclusive, but also allows people to contribute in spaces where they already feel comfortable.

As Box 3.12 illustrates, in mixed research teams, stepping into another researcher's world can be both expansive and enriching. These experiences open up perspectives, strengthen mutual respect, and demonstrate the breadth of lived knowledge within the research team.

> **Box 3.12: Community researcher reflections – stepping into new worlds**
>
> When the research project started, I had only recently started to get involved with community-based activities. I'm a rather introverted person, so I tended to keep to myself. However, the project required a lot of fieldwork; either with set groups or with random volunteers passing by our pop-ups. By no means was this easy for me, but it was a very enriching experience and I'm so happy I did it. Research for me usually means wedding myself to google for a few hours, but instead I was out talking to people, hearing about their experiences, and sharing my own. Our first session was with a Chinese community group in Lambeth, and it absolutely opened my eyes to how much fun these sessions could be. They were so friendly and happy to share parts of not only themselves, but also their culture and traditions. They even gifted us a copy of a book they'd made, which chronicled the experiences of various Chinese immigrants coming to the UK. It's one of my favourite books on my shelf and a physical representation of how our project had a personal touch that made it great for bridging the gap between the gallery and the local community.
>
> *Adeolu Adeouye, Community Researcher, Dulwich Picture Gallery project*

We have also learnt a great deal about what makes fieldwork successful and where challenges arise – in general, the warmer the connection between the community researcher and participants, the more fruitful the session. Research works particularly well when community researchers are already embedded in the setting: part of the group or association, or connected through a friend, family member, or colleague. Community festivals and markets often provide a positive atmosphere for engagement, whereas cold approaches at farmers' or public markets can be less effective. And sometimes, despite careful preparation, the conditions simply aren't right: the weather is poor and people don't want to stop and talk; a venue allocates us to the 'side room' where nobody goes; or effort is put into setting up a session, but participants don't turn up. It is important to normalise these realities: not every session will 'work', and that is part of the process. However, as Box 3.13 shows, it is through the fieldwork that community researchers often find they really fall in love with the method.

> **Box 3.13: Community researcher reflections – discovering confidence in Participatory Action Research**
>
> My journey with PAR began in 2013, when I started as a community researcher and was trained to use PAR tools. The training lasted two consecutive weeks and introduced me to a completely new way of working. At first, I felt alienated – most of the training felt overwhelming and I struggled to keep up. My confidence was low, and participating felt daunting.
>
> However, things began to shift during the second week. Concepts started to click, even though I still felt behind. Susie Hay, our trainer, believed in us and encouraged us to begin delivering sessions in the community.
>
> Once I stepped into the field – facilitating discussions in community centres, libraries, and other local spaces – I discovered something powerful: I was naturally good at facilitating. My confidence soared, and everything I had learned during the training began to make sense. Working alongside my colleagues and engaging directly with communities on health-related issues helped me internalise the tools and techniques in a way that classroom learning hadn't.
>
> That's when I truly fell in love with PAR. I began shadowing Susie in her other local sessions, eager to learn more. For me, the more I engaged with the community, the more I could apply what I'd learned. I realised I'm someone who learns best through hands-on experience and that it's OK not to grasp everything during verbal training, because growth happens in practice.

> Susie became my mentor and, with her support, I took the next step: completing a Train the Trainer programme. It involved a lot of writing and wasn't always easy, especially since I was on maternity leave at the time. But Susie was always there, ready to offer advice and encouragement. I could tell she was proud when I completed and submitted my work.
>
> This journey has deeply shaped the work I do today. It instilled in me a passion for working with communities and affirmed my belief in experiential learning. It taught me that confidence can grow in unexpected ways, and that mentorship and real-world engagement are powerful catalysts for personal and professional development.
>
> Now, in 2025, I'm still in touch with Susie. We check in with each other from time to time, and I continue to carry forward the lessons and values she helped instil in me.
>
> *Anita Khalil, Community Researcher, Camden Council, PAR project*

Fieldwork support and reflection

As facilitators, we provide assistance in organising sessions and offer on-the-ground support during fieldwork as needed. Project managers handle logistics, while a WhatsApp group enables effective communication among all involved parties.

To promote data collection and reflection, we provide a template for observations that capture essential details such as the number of participants, demographic information, reflections on how the sessions went, and emerging themes and thoughts to guide our research moving forward. These sheets are stored alongside the populated research tools and are labelled for easy reference during analysis sessions.

Midway through the fieldwork period, we facilitate a reflection session using the H-Form tool to review research progress, discuss the ups and downs of the process, examine how the questions have evolved (adding to our Question Bank), and determine whether any adjustments are needed. As Box 3.14 illustrates, reflecting and adapting approaches are key to successful PAR fieldwork. An analysis session, employing the Rose-Bud-Thorn tool, helps us identify emerging themes and potential recommendations, enabling us to adapt our focus or explore specific topics in greater depth. We also assess any gaps in demographic groups or geographic communities and use the Timeline Tool to plan the second fieldwork phase, ensuring more comprehensive representation. All of these tools are explored in more depth in Chapter 4.

> **Box 3.14: Community researcher reflections – conversations that matter**
>
> I was surprised by how community research sparked conversations and uncovered information that had previously been considered taboo , even among close family and friends. I was having conversations that, outside of research, I would have never have had with people to whom I am very close. It was fascinating to observe how people responded differently to the same topic, and to discover disparities in healthcare access among people living less than 30 minutes apart. The research taught me that learning and adapting is vital – what resonates with one participant may not work for another. It underscored the need for better public health outreach and enhanced my communication, critical thinking, and data-collection abilities.
>
> *Imogen Vowden, Community Researcher, Your Need to Know Campaign*
>
> My experience as a community researcher has been rewarding. It enabled me to gain inspiration and insight into various women's lives. Discussing gynaecological health in an informal setting hopefully will shape the future direction of women's healthcare.
>
> *Christiana Joseph, Community Researcher, You Need to Know Campaign*

Collaborative data analysis and reporting

Involving community researchers in data analysis has been a relatively recent practice in our projects. Traditionally, we collected data from community researchers and conducted the analysis ourselves, later incorporating their feedback and suggestions. However, recognising the benefits of maintaining a collaborative approach throughout the entire research process, we now actively engage community researchers in the analysis phase.

Positionality plays a crucial role in qualitative data analysis, as researchers' backgrounds inevitably shape their understanding of the phenomena being studied. It is essential to acknowledge that researchers are not mere observers, but active participants in the research process, and their positionality shapes their understanding of the phenomena being studied (England 1994). In collaborative data analysis with community researchers, diverse perspectives stemming from varied positionalities can enrich the interpretation of the data. By involving community members in the analysis process, we create an opportunity to challenge and expand our own understanding, which may otherwise be limited by our personal biases and experiences.

Key benefits of collaborative data analysis include the following:

1. **Shared ownership:** Encourages a sense of responsibility and investment in the research outcomes among all participants.
2. **Rigorous analysis:** The need to justify coding decisions to the entire team fosters transparency and challenges individual biases.
3. **Skills development:** Community researchers learn valuable data analysis techniques, expanding their research capabilities.

Our collaborative data analysis approach has been influenced by user-centred research methods from the service design field, particularly through our work with the Design Council (Design Council n.d.) We have adapted their step-by-step process for analysing large amounts of data, which provides structure and facilitates progress (see Chapter 4).

While data analysis can be challenging (see Box 3.15), the sense of collective achievement gained from making sense of the data outweighs the temporary fatigue. This collaborative process results in a clearer understanding of the research findings and the potential recommendations for change.

> **Box 3.15: Analysis isn't for everyone**
>
> In a recent project involving young people in Hackney, the young minds of the community researchers completed the analysis task in record time. Their thinking was rapid and very agile; they saw the links between themes and created a network of thoughts which they used as the basis of a report and presentation. We tried the same approach with an older group of volunteers about a subject very close to their hearts and we got horribly bogged down in the detail of individual experiences. At the end of a day, we hadn't even nearly finished and were all very tired. The experience is not one the volunteers would wish to repeat!

Action: moving towards change

Reporting and feedback

As part of our analysis process, we encourage community researchers to review their findings and develop recommendations for client organisations or commissioners. We then carefully consider the best methods to share research findings and gather feedback from the community on proposed actions and solutions. Over the years, we have adopted four approaches:

1. **Written reports:** We work together to compile a comprehensive report outlining the research findings, details on methodology and fieldwork, training provided, recommendations, and suggested actions.
2. **Visual illustrations or artwork:** In collaboration with talented artists such as Ada Jusic, Sarah Hoyle, and Kohenoor Kamal, we translate our key findings and takeaways into visual illustrations or artwork that can be easily shared with all research participants.
3. **Celebration events:** We organise a celebration event, such as the one set out in Box 3.16, inviting all project participants, decision makers, and stakeholders to share research findings and proposed actions. We also utilise feedback tools (see Chapter 4) to gather feedback on the presented ideas. This approach ensures a feedback loop with participants, enabling them to understand the research

journey, review the findings, and provide valuable input on the viability and relative importance of proposed recommendations.
4. **Creative approaches:** We have recently expanded our creative output beyond visual illustrations and songs. We continue to explore new artistic mediums, such as poetry and dance. These creative methods help us share our findings in more engaging, accessible formats. Box 3.17 highlights the experience of collaborating with a playwright as a way to bring to life research findings as part of an arts and heritage audience research project with the National Trust.

As a final step, we consolidate the feedback received into our report and develop an action plan, which is shared with our clients and commissioners.

Box 3.16: Brown Bag Lunch on the Aberfeldy estate

A community research project that looked at the issue of health, and specifically diabetes, in the Aberfeldy estate in East London had identified many barriers to accessing healthy food. The validation event was publicised in the area, invitations were extended widely, and it was held in a community centre at lunchtime when both professionals and the community might be free to attend. The event was entitled 'Brown Bag Lunch', with every person given a brown bag with a copy of the findings as well as fruit and other healthy eating-themed small gifts. All those present looked at ways of overcoming barriers and finding solutions using the tools together at the lunch tables, as well as enjoying a good hearty and healthy meal at a fun and productive event.

Box 3.17: Creative collaborator reflections – bringing paintings to life at Petworth House

The idea of bringing one of the paintings in the collection to life was an attempt to help visitors engage with the art in a more dynamic way. We chose the portrait of Catherine 'Kitty' Fisher, later Mrs. Norris (d. 1767) by Sir Joshua Reynolds, partly because it can get lost among other fine artworks and partly because of the fascinating stories associated with her life.

The online caption for the painting on the National Trust website reads:

> Kitty Fisher was a friend of Reynolds', and had a reputation as a courtesan, but on 9 November 1766 she married John Norris, MP, of Hempsted Manor, Benenden, Kent, who was MP for Rye 1762–1774. She died at Bath four months later, at the age of about twenty-six, 'a victim to cosmetics' (or smallpox), and was buried 'in her best dress' on 23 Mar 1767.

By 1760, a pamphlet addressed to her by 'Simon Trusty' claimed: 'Your Lovers are the Great Ones of the Earth, and your Admirers are the Mighty; they never approach you but, like Jove, in a shower of Gold.' Her voracity was notorious, and when Casanova met her in London in 1764, covered in diamonds and waiting to go to a ball, he was told that she had once clapped a £20 note into a bread-and-butter sandwich and consumed it.

But that information isn't immediately available to a visitor seeing the painting on the wall for the first time.

We arranged for an actor to portray Kitty, wearing the same costume and adopting the same pose as the painting, holding a letter. When the audience was in position, she 'came to life', telling her story both as the original sitter and as an observer of the house who has seen visitors come and go over the years.

This approach operated on several levels: it added a personal dimension to what might otherwise feel like historical biography, encouraged empathy, and captured audience attention in a different way. It allowed us to share information about both the artist and the subject, and to draw connections between their historical period and the present day.

> It was also an effective way to convey key research findings: visitors had reported feeling overwhelmed by the scale of Petworth House and the multitude of attractions. The performance offered an interpretive layer, helping visitors engage with a single painting and its story beyond the written interpretation materials provided.
>
> *Theresa Gooda, Creative Collaborator, Petworth House project*

Enacting change

Enacting change is often the most challenging aspect of PAR projects. While community research can generate rich insights and build local capacity, translating findings into concrete action is rarely straightforward.

Pain et al (2011) remind us that PAR is 'messy, political and contingent' – the move from knowledge to change depends not only on the commitment of community researchers but also on the willingness of institutions, funders and other stakeholders to share power and resources. Similarly, Kindon, Pain and Kesby (2007) stress that structural change is usually 'slow and uneven', and that PAR may be better at influencing relationships, awareness and practice at local levels than at shifting entrenched systems.

Others highlight that the 'stickiness' of change comes from both sides: institutions may be reluctant to alter existing practices, while communities themselves face deep-rooted inequalities, competing priorities, and limited resources, which can make action difficult to sustain (Cornwall and Jewkes 1995; Cahill 2007).

The following case studies illustrate these tensions: some show how meaningful change can occur when organisations commit to joint ownership of actions, while others reveal how even with strong research and engagement, action may falter.

Client-driven projects

In the most successful cases, clients take the findings and recommendations from PAR projects seriously and act upon them immediately. These clients have usually commissioned the projects with a clear purpose in mind and are genuinely invested in bringing about positive change. They view the work as more than a superficial exercise and are committed to making tangible improvements to their practices, policies, or processes. An example of an impactful client-driven PAR project is shown in Box 3.18.

> **Box 3.18: Participatory Action Research to support action on health and wellbeing at work**
>
> We worked with an Estate Services Team on a PAR project exploring health and wellbeing in the workplace at a large housing association in East London. Frontline workers identified barriers to using employer benefits such as health checks, including lack of clear information, form-filling difficulties linked to literacy challenges, and financial pressures around dental and optical care. Broader wellbeing issues were also raised: reliance on cheap junk food, the impact of long and expensive commutes, dog fouling and antisocial behaviour in the community, and low self-esteem due to feeling looked down on by other staff.
>
> What made this project successful was the immediate response of the management team. They openly acknowledged the issues, provided feedback on suggested actions, and, through an action-focused PAR session, committed to joint ownership of solutions. By incorporating these into workplace policies, both workers and managers saw evidence of accountability and commitment, giving the recommendations real traction.

Community-driven projects

Another type of project that has the potential to create change is one where communities themselves take ownership of the findings and act upon them. The success of these initiatives often relies on grassroots funding approaches, which empower communities to access the resources they need to implement change at the local level. By taking a bottom-up approach, these projects enable community members to work together and address the challenges they face directly. Box 3.19 highlights how, through participatory funding, the solutions to issues identified through a PAR project were designed and implemented by community members themselves. In contrast, Box 3.20 shows how change can be 'sticky' and even when the community has good actionable ideas without the resources behind them they cannot see them through.

> **Box 3.19: Neighbourhood Approaches to Loneliness**
>
> The Joseph Rowntree Foundation Neighbourhood Approaches to Loneliness Programme used PAR to develop community-driven strategies to reduce loneliness in four diverse areas. The programme recruited community researchers and worked in partnership with local organisations to develop activities that widened social networks and encouraged interaction across different ages and backgrounds.
>
> Community researchers set up a variety of initiatives, including walking groups, film clubs, parent-led stay-and-play sessions, pop-up summer cafés, and community cultural markets. Evaluation of the project in 2014 highlighted its impact on individuals and communities, and identified lessons for similar programmes:
>
> The programme had a transformative effect on many participants, helping them gain confidence, self-worth, and emotional intelligence. Some participants achieved tangible outcomes, such as returning to college or employment, while many others acquired new skills and capabilities that strengthened their engagement in the community.
>
>> I feel really lucky to be involved in this project ... I've really got to know [the parents] and I've seen how they have developed through working with us and doing the project. I've seen changes in those women which are phenomenal; two years ago those women were not the

same women they are now. (Children's Centre worker, suburban area, York)

I had certain predictions but I didn't think that it would be as in depth and developed the way it has. It's fantastic the sorts of things that are coming out. (Padma, community researcher, inner-city area, Bradford)

[I have learnt] ... to be a lot more confident, to be able to speak to people. It's helped me in my job really ... it enables me to approach people and, you know, changes your whole aspect. (Robert, community researcher, rural area, Bradford)

According to the evaluation report, the community research approach empowered local residents to take the initiative in developing activities for themselves and their neighbours. In many cases, these small teams of residents continued to run initiatives with little or no external support, embedding new social opportunities into the fabric of their communities (Collins and Wrigley 2014).

Box 3.20: A green space with potential, but no action

In a PAR project on type 2 diabetes prevention, we worked with a wide range of local partners and community researchers to explore barriers to active lifestyles and healthy eating. The focal point of the area was a large green space at the heart of the neighbourhood, surrounded by social housing. Many residents saw it as a potential hub for family exercise, outdoor activity, and food growing.

However, issues such as antisocial behaviour, litter, and dangerous objects left people feeling unsafe and prevented the space from being used as intended. Although funding was available and a local community group had offered to support a clean-up, longstanding problems such as litter and dog fouling persisted. Co-production in this instance did not translate into practical action, and the opportunity to transform the green space was not realised.

Extended collaborative projects

A third type of project that can lead to tangible change involves an ongoing partnership between community researchers and organisations. In these cases, organisations commit to involving researchers in the implementation phase, utilising their expertise and knowledge gained from the research project. Researchers work closely with organisations to develop solutions, products, or services that directly address the findings and recommendations from the research. This collaborative approach can help ensure that the outcomes of the project are translated into meaningful and lasting change.

Box 3.21: Better Births – embedding community researchers

We collaborated with UCL's Partners Better Births project, aiming to enhance maternity care and outcomes for women and their families in North Central London Boroughs. We brought together a diverse team of community researchers who had recently experienced the maternity care system. Our team received comprehensive training in community research tools and techniques, enabling them to conduct fieldwork within their respective communities and gather valuable insights, particularly concerning birth and postnatal care.

The research uncovered powerful perspectives on women's experiences, revealing areas needing improvement. Consequently, our community researcher team developed a training course focusing on the significance of active listening and kindness in healthcare interactions. The research also continued, emphasising the unique experiences of Black and minoritised women who were revealed to receive different treatment through the research. As the project evolved, community researchers assumed roles as

> Patient Involvement Partners within the hospital trust, ensuring ongoing collaboration and progress.
>
> A key factor contributing to this project's success was UCL Partners directly employing community researchers, which strengthened their capacity to drive meaningful change. By embedding legacy roles within the project, we ensured that community researchers remained engaged, and change happened in a meaningful and sustainable way.

Evaluation: reflecting, refining, and redirecting Participatory Action Research initiatives

Evaluation is a crucial component of any PAR project, but it can be particularly challenging. Literature on PAR consistently highlights the difficulty of assessing impact, especially in small, project-by-project initiatives commissioned by different clients. Common barriers include limited budgets, short timelines, and the complex, often gradual nature of change that PAR seeks to enable (Minkler 2005; Baum et al 2006).

In practice, we also find it hard to prioritise and resource evaluation systematically. While reflection is embedded in day-to-day project activities – through team discussions, mid-project reviews, and iterative analysis – it is more difficult to step back and assess the broader impact, value, and learning across multiple PAR projects.

To address this, we have employed a range of evaluation approaches in our PAR work:

Embedded evaluation

All our PAR projects incorporate evaluation tools directly into workshops and fieldwork as a matter of course. These tools, such as observation sheets, the H-Form, Rose-Bud-Thorn exercises, Evaluation Betty, the Pizza Pie tool, and the Reflective Timeline, allow us, as a team, to capture insights about progress, emerging themes, and immediate outcomes for participants and community researchers. We also use these tools to gather feedback and adapt approaches as needed, ensuring that reflection is an ongoing, integral part of the research process. This approach is participant-led, drawing on the tradition of participatory evaluation, in which outcomes and evaluation criteria are shaped by community researchers themselves rather than imposed by external professional or academic evaluators (Worthen, Veale, and Wessells 2019).

Independent evaluators

While not without its tensions, some PAR projects have involved working with independent evaluators to bring in additional capacity, resources, and an external perspective in order to capture broader organisational and sectoral learning. As Newman (2008) explores, there are inherent tensions in this work between the desire to be participatory and the reality of evaluation processes that serve multiple – and at times conflicting – objectives. This is especially the case when project outputs and outcomes are defined by external funding bodies, or when evaluators draw on methodologies that are not themselves participatory, such as conventional quantitative or qualitative approaches. However, as Box 3.22 illustrates, when ethical commitments are aligned and evaluation is integrated into the process from the outset, collaboration with an independent evaluator can add real value.

Box 3.22: Independent evaluation and action learning in the Past for the Present project

The Past for the Present project at Dulwich Picture Gallery, funded by the Esmée Fairbairn Foundation, explored how historic paintings in the collection could resonate with contemporary lives. Using PAR, community researchers worked with curators, educators, and artists to experiment with new ways of interpreting and presenting the collection. The project aimed to connect past and present in ways that felt relevant to diverse audiences and to generate fresh perspectives on the gallery's role in contemporary society.

An independent evaluator, Alis Templeton, was engaged from the start to integrate evaluation into the process and ensure that learning extended beyond the project team. Alis designed participatory evaluation methods, including workshops and action learning sets, which created structured opportunities for reflection and dialogue.

The evaluation captured the impact of the PAR strand on multiple levels. Within the gallery, it informed the development of a new gallery display, influenced both online and in-person programming, and helped shape a long-term curatorial plan. Beyond the gallery, the evaluation also generated transferable insights, providing a platform for shared learning across the sector and helping other organisations consider how PAR can support innovation in audience research and local community engagement.

Systematic evaluation

Finally, when multiple PAR projects are undertaken within the same organisation or network, a more systematic evaluation approach can be used to identify patterns, cumulative learning, and longer-term impacts. This involves collecting data consistently across projects, tracking outcomes over time, and synthesising insights to inform organisational strategy, sector-level practice, and community impact. Evaluation results can also reveal new areas of inquiry or indicate the need for further exploration of existing topics, leading to additional projects that continue to engage community members in the research process. While resource-intensive, systematic evaluation can provide the strongest evidence for the value of PAR and help advocate for its continued support (see *3* for an example of this happening in practice).

Box 3.23: The Community Insights Programme – embedding Participatory Action Research in Tower Hamlets

The Community Insights Programme, a collaboration between Tower Hamlets Council and Tower Hamlets

Together, aimed to integrate community-led research into the development of policies and services across Tower Hamlets. This approach acknowledged the vital role community-led research plays in engaging local residents in service design, delivery, and evaluation, while fostering active partnerships with various local sectors. The network sought to build upon ten years of community research conducted in the borough for the public health team.

The programme successfully united a diverse group of organisations, including community researchers, groups, housing associations, voluntary sector organisations, council departments, and universities, all sharing an interest in community research and actively practising it. It also established a community insights repository and a pool of in-house community insights researchers.

The Community Insights Programme resulted in several notable outcomes, including increased awareness, understanding, and utilisation of community research by service providers in Tower Hamlets, a greater community voice and ownership in the development of local services through the engagement of 750 local people by community researchers in the development of the Tower Hamlets Community Plan, and enhanced skills, capacity, and work opportunities for community researchers.

Embedding a community research team within the local council was found to be effective in extending community research beyond public health, fostering cross-department collaboration, and raising its profile. Additionally, employing and training community researchers as an in-house resource, with competitive pay, flexible working conditions, and comprehensive training and support, is an equitable model that could be replicated elsewhere.

While many of our projects incorporate reflective and embedded evaluation tools, and some benefit from external evaluators or systematic approaches, there remains a wider challenge: the lack of consistent, joined-up evaluation across PAR practice. Too often, evaluation is fragmented, project-specific, and constrained by limited resources. What is needed is institutional support for evaluation that goes beyond individual initiatives, enabling us to advocate for the impact and value of PAR, to share key learning across contexts, and to build a stronger collective understanding of what best practice looks like. A more integrated approach to evaluation would not only enhance the credibility of PAR but would also strengthen its potential as a driver of social change.

Participatory Action Research as an evaluation tool

To conclude this section, it is worth emphasising that PAR can function as an evaluation tool in its own right. Beyond being a research approach, it offers a way to centre user voices in the evaluation of community-based initiatives. By actively involving participants in defining what matters to them, PAR allows evaluation to be meaningful, relevant, and grounded in lived experience. This can be a powerful way to identify issues and improve community initiatives iteratively. It also supports the development of research skills within the community, enabling participants to go on and provide evaluation support in their own organisations and careers using participatory methods. Box 3.24 shows how community champions were upskilled in PAR so they could have an active role in the project evaluation.

> **Box 3.24: Reflections from a commissioner – upskilling community health champions in evaluative Participatory Action Research**
>
> We used participatory methods to evaluate the Health Trainers programme in Tower Hamlets in 2013/2014. We needed an approach that was inclusive, fun, and engaging. As a commissioner, it was important that the process felt less like extracting information and more like genuinely understanding what brought service users to the service, and whether outcomes aligned with their expectations. PAR seemed like the perfect fit, and we commissioned Shortwork to evaluate the community lifestyle sessions.

The evaluation process was a great success, though we did encounter some teething issues. The Health Trainers were initially hesitant about the process; it felt very different from the usual form-filling or survey-based evaluations. They also struggled with the logistics of consent and arranging for service users to stay after their sessions to fully engage with the facilitators. Despite these challenges, the process led to rich discussions with service users, generating valuable insights about what was working well and where improvements were needed. For example, it became clear that segregated fitness sessions were important for women of all ethnicities to feel comfortable exercising, not just for women from global majority communities. We were also able to identify the characteristics of a high-quality community-based session, which later informed our quality assurance processes.

By the end of the evaluation, the Health Trainers had come to appreciate the value of genuine participation and recognising service users as experts in their own lives. They expressed a desire to use participatory methods to evaluate their own sessions and other aspects of frontline work – an impressive skill set for the Public Health workforce and a sustainable legacy of PAR for the borough.

Radhika Puri, Commissioner, Tower Hamlets Public Health

Conclusion

This chapter has set out the ethos and guiding lights behind our approach to PAR, as well as the key stages we move through in our projects: Partnering, Preparation, Research, Action, Evaluation (and Repeat). We have tried to provide a route map for others so that practitioners, organisations, and community researchers have a sense of the journey and the tools available at different points along the way. However, what emerges clearly is that PAR is not a linear method, but a dynamic and adaptive process that requires openness to uncertainty, space for reflection, and the ability to pivot when circumstances change.

The case studies and reflections we've shared highlight both the promise and the challenges of working in this way. We have seen how creativity and collaboration can generate new forms of knowledge and open up possibilities for action. At the same time, we have acknowledged the 'stickiness' of change, the difficulties of sustaining momentum, and the barriers to embedding evaluation. These tensions are not failures but reminders of the complexity of doing participatory work in real-world contexts, where multiple agendas and limited resources are always at play.

Crucially, the process of PAR is as valuable as its outputs. The practices of training and upskilling, questioning, reflecting, and adapting strengthen communities and organisations, build individual and group capacity, and foster trust, even when immediate change is partial or slow. Across the projects discussed in this chapter, what stands out is the cumulative impact of these processes: community researchers gain new skills, confidence, and opportunities; groups of participants deepen their understanding and agency; and communities benefit from strengthened networks, shared knowledge, and collective action.

As we move on to the next chapter, which explores the tools in more detail, we invite readers to hold onto this understanding of PAR as both structured and improvisational: a process that relies on practical techniques, but also thrives on curiosity, creativity, and persistence.

4

The tools

In this chapter, we delve into specific diagramming, visual, and creative tools essential for structuring, guiding, and capturing conversations during PAR fieldwork. These tools are not only utilised by researchers in various participatory settings but also form the suite of methods community researchers learn during their training. These tools complement the participatory techniques and methodologies discussed in Chapter 3. While not exhaustive, as many practitioners employ various creative and diagramming methodologies in their work, they represent a curated selection of approaches we have grown familiar with and found valuable in our projects.

We begin by examining the sequencing of these tools, which aids community researchers in designing their fieldwork. The tools are presented in sections that align with the various stages of PAR: exploration, focused conversations, analysis, action planning and evaluation.

Our aim is to provide a practical guide to using these tools, filling a gap in the existing literature by drawing inspiration from the works of Robert Chambers and other influential figures in the field. By offering a clear and accessible explanation of these methods, we hope to equip readers with the knowledge and resources necessary to effectively engage in PAR initiatives.

As discussed in Chapter 3, the effectiveness of these tools depends on proficient facilitation and open questioning skills. Community researchers prepare topics beforehand, using the Questions Bank and fieldwork guide for reference, while tailoring the specific questions based on participant engagement.

By employing open-ended questions and the six 'little helpers' (who? what? where? why? when? and how?), researchers can delve deeper into topics that generate interest among participants, while avoiding those that do not resonate. This approach ensures a dynamic and participant-centred experience that adapts to the unique needs and interests of each fieldwork session (Jones 1995).

Tool sequencing

To make the chapter easily navigable for readers, we will structure it by categorising the visual tools into five primary stages: exploration, focused conversations, analysis, action planning, and evaluation. These categories reflect the different purposes and functions the tools serve throughout the research process. However, it is important to recognise that many of these tools can be adapted and used in multiple stages, offering flexibility in their application.

- **Tools for exploration:** This section will introduce tools that initiate discussions and gather initial broad insights, such as maps (including body maps), Timelines, and Graffiti Walls. These tools help capture the community's or group's knowledge or opinions of a broad issue or theme.
- **Tools for focused discussions:** In this section, we will explore tools that facilitate a more in-depth analysis of issues, including H-Forms, Spider Diagrams and Causal Impact Diagrams. These tools enable participants to focus the discussion and deepen their understanding of the issues at hand.
- **Tools for analysis:** This section sets out the tools that we use to facilitate collaborative data analysis with the community researcher team. The tools enable the coding and thematic clustering of research data collected during the fieldwork, and support key findings and recommendations to emerge.
- **Tools for action planning:** These tools aid action planning, such as Matrix Ranking, Criteria Ranking, and Beany Counters. As the discussion progresses towards taking action or assessing impact, these tools prove to be particularly useful.
- **Tools for evaluation:** Finally, we explore tools that support reflection and evaluation through the process, including Evaluation Betty and the Pizza Pie tool. These are used and embedded

throughout our PAR projects to capture learning and impacts, and to gather feedback to support iteration in our approaches.

Please note that some tools are applicable to multiple stages of the research process. In these cases, we will discuss the tool in detail once and indicate its applicability to other stages where relevant.

Tools for exploration

These exploratory tools are invaluable in the early stages of research, as they enable participants to delve into broad topic areas with open minds. By encouraging individuals to take their own direction and bring attention to potentially relevant aspects that may have otherwise been overlooked, these tools foster a comprehensive understanding of the subject matter. The use of more open, free-form, arts-based tools not only promotes individual reflection but also encourages creative thinking and alternative perspectives. This approach ensures that all participants can contribute meaningfully, regardless of their literacy or numeracy levels. It's important to remember that not everyone feels comfortable with open-ended creative tools. At times, it can be valuable to encourage people to step slightly outside their comfort zones. However, if these tools clearly don't suit the group, be flexible – adapt the plan or set it aside to better meet people's needs. By avoiding the limitations imposed by tools that provide more structure and narrow conversations, these exploratory methods help to uncover a wide range of insights and lay the foundations for more focused research in later stages.

Maps

Mapping (see Figure 4.1) is a versatile and essential tool in PAR, as it enables people to express their experiences and perceptions of their environment. Various types of maps can be employed for different purposes, making them adaptable to diverse communities and contexts. Some common types include the following:

- **Social and cultural maps:** These reveal the social fabric of a community or society, including cultural aspects (Duxbury, Garrett-Petts, and MacLennan 2020).

- **Linguistic maps:** These identify the diverse languages spoken (and written) in a community (Gaiser and Matras 2021).
- **Power maps:** These identify key stakeholders, decision makers, and institutions that shape a place or neighbourhood, often focusing on a particular issue or concern.
- **Health equity maps:** These highlight disparities in health outcomes within a community.
- **Community asset and hazard maps:** These showcase the strengths and dangers faced by a community (Alevizou, Alexiou, and Zamenopoulos 2016; Sullivan-Wiley, Short Gianotti, and Casellas Connors 2019).
- **Mobility maps**: These represent people's movements within a particular area, highlighting the destinations they visit, the frequency of their trips, the modes of transportation they use, and the barriers faced during door-to-door journeys (Evans 2009).
- **Citizen science maps:** These allow members of the public to collect and report citizen science information, for example, geographic and ecological data (Newman et al 2010).
- **Historical maps:** These illustrate how an area has changed over time, providing valuable insights into its development and evolution (Lichtenstein et al 2020).
- **Potential or ideal maps:** These visualise what a community could or should be like – for instance, to inform town planning (Brown, Sanders, and Reed 2018).

Participatory mapping can be powerful in, for example, documenting a cultural and legal entitlement to land (Bryan 2011; Rye and Kurniawan 2017; Rainforest Foundation 2020), identifying place-based issues such as environmental degradation (Chambers 2006), and supporting the interests of particular groups such as people living with disabilities, children and the young, and older people.

Professionally produced maps can be part of the PAR process, with community researchers taking a role in collecting the data mapped (Schultz 2006; Corburn et al 2013). The emergence of new technologies, including geographic information systems (GIS) and more recent accessible and user-friendly bespoke and off-the peg online maps (Lichtenstein et al 2020; Gaiser and

Figure 4.1: Mapping place

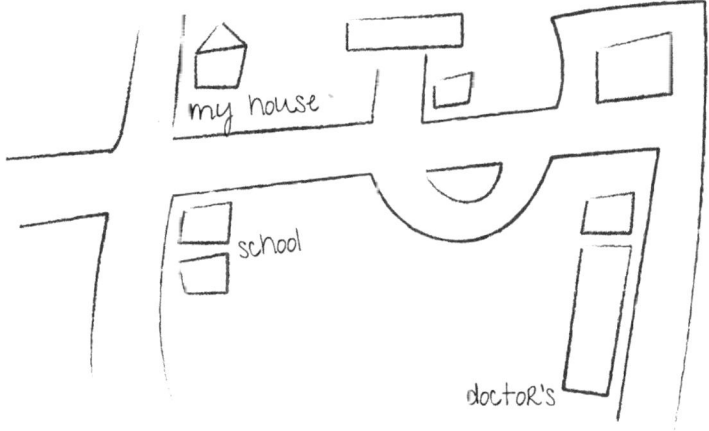

Matras 2021), have enabled more people to engage in map making (Cochrane and Corbett 2020).

In the context of PAR projects focusing on gathering qualitative data about people's experiences and perspectives, hand-drawn maps created by research participants themselves can play a vital role. Place maps often involve creative techniques like drawing, painting, and collage to visually represent a place, allowing participants to express their unique experiences and understanding of their neighbourhood. Light-touch, drama-based methods can also be employed, for example, by asking participants to imagine a giant map on the floor of a room, and asking them to stand on a location that holds personal significance to them. Physical mapping can also take place in the community, as explored in .

> **Box 4.1: In-situ mapping in Barton upon Humber**
>
> Councillors in Barton upon Humber were receiving a lot of complaints about children and young people in the town behaving in an antisocial way, hanging out in bus stops and the like.
>
> The Humber and Wolds Community Council undertook a project to find out why this was happening and to hear

from the young people about what was needed locally that would remedy the situation. Councillors expressed great concern that they would be asked for expensive facilities, like a new youth centre, and were very sceptical about what the outcomes of the research project would be. Young people undertook community research training and fieldwork was carried out with their peers in the town.

The young people adapted the mapping tool in a most creative way: they made 'flags' (that is, cocktail sticks with labels attached) and stuck one in each patch of dog excrement on the football pitch. The impact of this was visible for all (including the Councillors) to see and the message was clear – we want a football pitch without dog poo on it. They also pointed out that the goal posts were regularly taken down outside school hours, and consequently they couldn't play informally themselves.

People in authority and/or those with control of funding can be hostile to PAR projects which ask people 'what they want', saying it will cost the earth or it won't be possible because of a lack of resources. We and others have often found that if the community is asked for solutions, these will also be modest; people living with disadvantage and lack of money are often the first to understand that not everything is affordable. Better lighting, litter bins and provision of dog poo bags are often cheap options. By being asked at all for their opinions, people will also feel they are being listened to. As highlighted here, lack of trust and respect for young people on the part of older members of the community is frequently encountered. Community research can help bridge this gap and foster understanding between generations.

Contrary to traditional cartographic mapping, participatory approaches often yield unique and personalised representations that deviate from realistic geographical maps. In fact, the term 'map' may elicit unease among participants, who might prefer a more inviting prompt like 'draw your community'. Consequently, these participatory maps often emphasise particular aspects while omitting others, resulting in mental maps that illustrate an individual's subjective understanding of a place.

In our projects, we often invite participants to explore various themes in their maps. Examples include a cultural map of southeast London, which encourages individuals to highlight significant locations and experiences in their community (Adeouye et al 2023). Often, maps like these take the form of a journey and can highlight the people as well as places that are significant (Swords et al 2019). Another mapping approach focuses on smaller spaces, such as a map of an individual's experiences with energy-efficient retrofits in their home (Rezvani et al 2025).

Employing metaphors in mapping exercises allows participants to visualise and communicate complex ideas and experiences that may not have a distinct geographical representation. For instance, in a PAR project examining refugee women's experiences accessing services and support in the UK, we used the metaphor of a 'universe of support' to help participants depict different organisations and their influence on their lives. In this metaphorical map, participants represented various organisations as planets of differing sizes, symbolising their power and influence. The proximity of these planets to the participants' 'home planet' illustrated the responsiveness and helpfulness of each organisation.

Whether drawn or imaginary, gender, age, disability, ethnicity, and occupation will all affect the significant places that participants mark on a map. As a result, the same area may look very different because of the variety of ways in which people see things and the different things that matter to them. As a result, mapping can be particularly powerful for groups whose experiences of a neighbourhood or city are overlooked, particularly by those who make decisions about design, planning and public services. For example, mapping provided a way to explore children's perspectives of neighbourhood spaces (Ozbil Torun et al 2024), young people's views of youth services (Amsden and VanWynsberghe 2005), and gendered experiences of 'place' in the urban environment for street homeless women (Cook and Corbett 2019). In our experience, working on maps in mixed groups enables discussions to take place and allows people to see what's important to other people – including things they might not know about or use themselves.

At the onset of PAR projects, maps serve as valuable tools for various reasons:

1. **Icebreaker activities**: They can act as engaging 'icebreakers' that encourage participation and collaboration, as noted by Corburn et al (2013).
2. **Contextualisation**: They provide context for discussions, offering insights into participants' experiences and understanding of their environment.
3. **Facilitating understanding:** They help reveal differences and similarities in people's experiences, fostering a sense of community among researchers and participants.
4. **Fieldwork planning**: They can assist researchers in identifying key individuals and locations for research sessions.

Later on in the process, maps can be used to examine more deeply specific issues, revisit concerns, or plan for changes in certain areas. In this way, maps are dynamic and adaptable tools that support ongoing reflection and dialogue throughout the research process.

Figure 4.2: Body map

Body maps (see Figure 4.2) serve as valuable exploratory and creative tools in PAR projects. Utilising a variety of creative techniques, body maps allow participants to visually represent various aspects of their lives, bodies, and environments (Shah, Kambou, and Monahan 1999; Gastaldo et al 2012). Body maps have been widely used in a health context, for example, in exploring people's experience of living with particular health conditions (Ludlow 2014; Jokela-Pansini and Greenhough 2024; Morgan and Bambanani Women's Group 2003), as a way to identify pain and discomfort (Michigan Medicine 2024), and to explore sigma and taboo (Morgan and Bambanani Women's Group 2003), as well as some of the environmental impacts on health – for example, in the workplace (Keith and Brophy 2004). Body maps have also been used to explore people's experience of change and transition in their lives – for instance, undocumented migrants, refugees, and people seeking asylum (Gastaldo et al 2012; O'Brien and Charura 2023), as well as older people in care homes (Smith et al 2023).

In the realm of qualitative PAR, body maps offer a powerful platform for participants to share their personal narratives, uncover hidden experiences, and facilitate open dialogue within the community (Gastaldo et al 2012). Being a visual-based method, they also offer an alternative way of knowing and expressing experiences that complements traditional verbal or text-based approaches (Jager et al 2016). By engaging participants in the creative process, body maps can encourage more prolonged contemplation of the research topic (Bagnoli 2009). The benefits of body maps are particularly evident when working with specific groups, such as children, young people, individuals with language barriers, or those with limited literacy skills (Bagnoli 2009). Furthermore, body maps can foster a sense of empowerment among participants by providing a platform for self-expression and ownership over the representation of their experiences (Huss et al 2015).

Additionally, body maps can serve as an effective tool for communicating stories and raising awareness about important issues to a broader audience, for example, through formal installations or exhibitions of the art work produced (Brett-MacLean 2009; Jager et al 2016), helping to shed light on social injustices or inequalities, and contributing to campaigns for change.

At the start of a PAR project, body maps serve as a valuable tool in the training room in the following ways:

1. **Learning aid:** Helping community researchers to visualise their roles and responsibilities as facilitators, observers or anti-saboteurs. For instance, participants can draw their 'perfect facilitator', highlighting positive traits, or the 'world's worst facilitator' to generate laughter and reflection on undesirable qualities.
2. **Feedback tool:** Serving as an evaluation tool for gathering feedback on sessions, using broad categories such as 'heart', 'head', 'bag', and 'bin' to express what they liked or didn't like, potential improvements, and the session's impact. Encouraging community researchers to use body mapping in their own fieldwork sessions can help generate reflection and learning.

During the fieldwork, body maps are useful in opening up exploratory discussions around an issue or topic such as the following:

1. **Personal experiences:** Body mapping is useful for investigating the experiential aspects of a topic under study. For instance, it can be employed to better understand how participants feel when walking through an art gallery or living in poorly insulated, underheated homes, capturing their physical and emotional experiences.
2. **Comparisons and differences:** Body mapping can highlight the differences between people's experience, and the impact of, for example, disability, age, race, or gender. Box 4.2 shows how body maps can be used to draw out shared experiences of people in similar roles or positions within a community.

> **Box 4.2: Body mapping to explore the realities of social leadership**
>
> We used a body mapping exercise to explore the personal and professional journeys of leaders in community-based

social enterprises and charities. Each participant was given a pre-drawn body outline and invited to personalise it, turning it into a visual representation of themselves as leaders.

Key steps included the following:

- Customising the body outline: Participants added clothes, accessories, and other details to reflect their individuality.
- Reflecting on their journey: Using thought bubbles, they noted the experiences – both positive and negative – that shaped their path as leaders.
- Creating symbols and slogans: Each participant designed a symbol and accompanying slogan to represent their identity and values as a leader.
- Identifying support structures: Using armchair and cushion stickers, participants mapped out the people, institutions, and resources that had supported them, as well as additional support they needed.
- Visualising the future: Arrows at the feet of the figure allowed participants to chart their next steps in their leadership journey.

This exercise offered rich insights into the challenges, resilience, and motivations of social enterprise leaders. It enabled participants to externalise and share complex experiences, reflect on the support that sustains them, and visualise their ongoing development. Many reported that seeing their journey mapped out in this way made abstract experiences tangible, helping them recognise both achievements and areas for growth, while fostering connections with other leaders undertaking similar journeys.

Timelines

Like body maps, timelines (see Figure 4.3) are valuable tools for capturing the complexities of personal and communal histories

Figure 4.3: Timeline

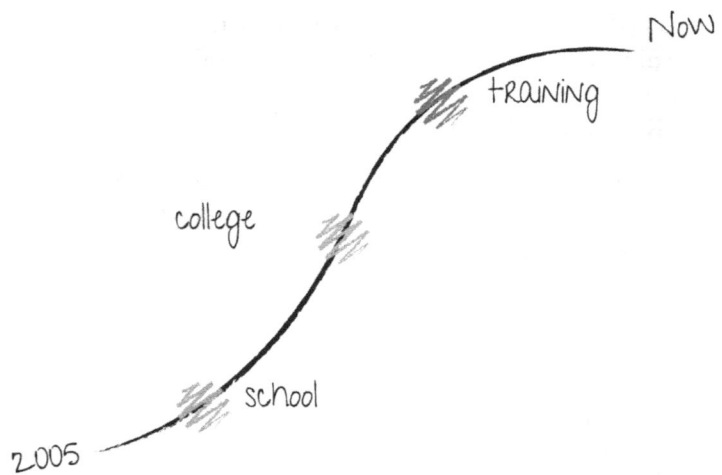

in PAR projects (Bagnoli 2009). These visual representations empower participants by enabling them to construct and share their unique stories without constraints (Adriansen 2012; Hurtubise and Joslin 2023).

Timelines take on various forms, including sketches, cartoon strips, and metaphorical depictions (Berends 2011). They can also be modelled in three-dimensions using materials such as clay, feathers, string, and pipecleaners rather than drawn. The use of 3D timelines can make the timeline tool more accessible for example to people with limited literacy or those who are blind or visually impaired (Thompson n.d.). Whether drawn and modelled, these versatile visuals chronologically display significant events, allowing participants to annotate and illustrate their meanings (Adriansen 2012). They can also encompass various timespans, ranging from daily activities affecting physical activity levels to factors impacting education over a school week, or even the effects of maternity care access over nine months. Furthermore, they can illustrate the evolution of a community across decades or document a person's entire lifetime (Adriansen 2012). These adaptable tools can be single or multilayered, capturing diverse experiences and contexts, such as social or economic changes within a community (Adriansen 2012). They can also be layered with drawing and symbols which represent emotions, or evaluate experiences as positive or negative.

In the health sphere, timelines help understand personal experiences with illnesses and healthcare services (Berends 2011; Sheridan, Chamberlain, and Dupuis 2011; Deng Deng et al 2019; Hurtubise and Joslin 2023). Furthermore, they have been used to engage marginalised groups, like immigrant women and street-involved youth (Kolar et al 2015).

Timelines can also be used in a group context to document change in a community over time. The process of generating a group timeline can shake out differences in the ways in which people see change and the significance of those changes in their communities over time. These might be changes in services and facilities, but could be other things like perceptions of the environment as a consequence of physical changes to it, or the behaviour of people in it.

Timelines generate valuable insights through recollection, sequencing, and meaning making while serving as a tool for reflection and decision making (Berends 2011). This participatory approach can foster a sense of ownership over personal and collective stories, while also helping people to plan for the future by identifying changes they would like to see in their lives or in the lives of their community, in turn helping to highlight the steps that might need to happen to achieve that particular goal.

At the outset of PAR projects, timelines can serve as valuable tools in the following ways:

1. **Facilitate group familiarisation:** In training sessions, timelines can help participants understand the life events that led them to the project. However, trainers should exercise caution, as timelines may evoke strong emotions or difficult memories. It is crucial to create a safe space where participants only share what they feel comfortable with. Community researchers must have ample time to build their timelines individually, discuss them with a partner, and share general observations with the larger group focused on shared

experiences, differences, and valuable takeaways rather than detailed personal accounts. Box 4.4 shows how the sharing of personal stories via timelines can create common-ground and connection between people on the research team from different walks of life.
2. **Organise research and teamwork:** To complement the mapping tool, we encourage community researchers to utilise a timeline for planning their fieldwork sessions systematically, incorporating essential details to streamline logistics.

During the fieldwork phase, timelines can serve as an effective tool for the following:

1. **Conducting in-depth exploration:** Timelines are particularly useful when researching topics related to personal journeys, mobility, or experiences with specific health or community services. In our research on maternity care services, community researchers and participants embraced timelines as an impactful method, adding layers of detail and interpretation. This process allowed individuals to share their personal birth stories and healthcare system experiences, fostering a sense of relief and empowerment for those who felt their voices had been previously unheard. Similarly, as Box 4.3 shows, timelines proved to be a powerful tool for personal reflection on the SOS gangs project.
2. **Facilitating community researcher reflection:** Throughout the fieldwork phase, particularly at the midway point and near its conclusion, timelines can serve as a valuable tool for community researchers to look back on and learn from their conducted sessions. By documenting their feelings, successes, challenges, and potential improvements, researchers engage in reflective practice. This process encourages personal growth and adaptability while informing future research strategies and methods.

At the research project's conclusion, timelines can play a critical role in planning for action. They assist community researchers, the broader community, and influential stakeholders/sponsor organisations in visualising and coordinating next steps.

> **Box 4.3: The power of personal timelines**
>
> A young person took part in PAR training in a project about the experience of being a gang member in South London. He had been a gang member and served time in prison. He found the training suited him with its emphasis on drawing and using visual tools. For most of the time, he kept the hood of his top over his head. In the timeline exercise he chose to draw his life in a series of drawings – a cradle, a school, a gang, guns and knives, blood and, finally, a drawing of a gravestone (his own). He shared his timeline in the feedback session, removing his hood and declaring 'I drew my life today, and it's the first time I've looked at it'.

> **Box 4.4: The power of sharing stories**
>
> A training course in Limehouse, East London brought together a diverse group of people who got to know each other better through taking part and sharing. In the timeline exercise, an Eastern European woman (a parent using the Children's Centre) and a Muslim woman (who was a health worker) compared their timelines and their experiences of marriage: one a love marriage and the other an arranged marriage. They agreed that what they had in common was that they were both very happy in their marriages.

Graffiti wall

A graffiti wall is a flexible tool for gathering rich, authentic feedback from diverse participants. Developed in the user experience design world (Martin and Hanington 2012), graffiti walls have been adapted for use in PAR as a simple way to elicit ideas and opinions (Mathers 2010; Parme 2014). The method is not widely cited in the published literature, but is a tool that we use in community-based research projects outside academia on a regular basis.

Figure 4.4: Graffiti wall

The graffiti wall is essentially a temporary large-format canvas of paper, card, or cloth, with a key question or prompt written at the top, and space for participants to respond to that question through the free expression using writing and drawing, aided by coloured pens and other creative materials.

Graffiti walls are an excellent starting point for research projects due to their simplicity and adaptability. Their ease of facilitation makes them ideal for less experienced community researchers. They can be facilitated in groups, individually, or unattended, allowing participants to provide feedback anonymously if preferred.

These installations can be incorporated into 'pop-up' style stalls at existing community events or activities, enabling passers-by to participate quickly without engaging in more complex discussions. Graffiti walls can serve as semi-permanent displays in public venues like libraries or even toilets (Martin and Hanington 2012). This enables people to contribute even when a community researcher is not present, fostering participation in discussions that may involve sensitive or personal topics in quieter, less open spaces. In these contexts, photos of graffiti walls can be taken to document new comments and sketches, and are removed at the end of the research period, to be analysed, and compared, with other walls collected from other locations as part of the research project (Martin and Hanington 2012).

Graffiti walls are a valuable tool that can be used throughout the different stages of a project. At the beginning, graffiti walls are useful for the following purposes:

1. **Establishing collaborative practices:** In the training room, graffiti walls enable participants to collectively define and display the ground rules for working together. Graffiti walls also provide an area where participants can document ideas in a 'car park' or 'bike rack' that may not be relevant to the current discussion, but could be useful later on in the research process.
2. **Shaping and testing research questions:** Community researchers actively contribute to the graffiti wall by formulating, refining, and testing research questions based on their expertise and experiences. This collaborative approach ensures that the questions are relevant, meaningful, and grounded in the community's context. As the project evolves, community researchers can amend and update the research questions on the graffiti wall to reflect new insights and emerging priorities. As such, the graffiti wall serves as a working document that can be continuously amended and evolved as the research project progresses.

During the fieldwork stage of a research project, graffiti walls play an essential role in the following ways:

1. **Encouraging loose and open interpretations:** By providing an open canvas for ideas, graffiti walls allow participants to explore and express their unique perspectives on the research topic or question, including aspects that may initially seem unrelated or tangential.
2. **Categorising ideas in group settings:** In community researcher-facilitated sessions, graffiti walls allow participants

to categorise ideas displayed on the walls, often by 'clustering' sticky notes. This collaborative activity helps identify shared themes and topics, guiding the direction of future research sessions.

Later on in the research process, graffiti walls become valuable for generating a multitude of ideas or recommendations, often at a fast pace. As participants build upon each other's contributions, they can collectively explore potential solutions or areas of focus.

Tools for focused discussions

These tools are used later on in the research process to narrow down the research questions and explore specific elements identified using the exploratory tools in greater depth. They include more structured, diagrammatic tools which provide a clear framework for conversations and rely on closer facilitation by community researchers who may need to guide participants through the tool in question. Though more focused, these tools are flexible, allowing researchers to explore different questions, build on discussions, and help research participants examine an issue or question from a different perspective.

The H-Form

The H-Form, or 'Rugby Post Form' method, was developed by Andy Inglis in 1997 to support local communities in Somalia with monitoring and evaluating local environmental management (Guy and Inglis 1999). It has subsequently been adapted and used in many contexts, often in workshop settings which bring together a range of stakeholders into one space in order to explore consensus as whether outlier options on a range of issues including sustainable food systems (Steps Centre 2016), improving public participation in decision making relating to science and technology (Hunsberger and Kenyon 2008), engaging young people in the evaluation of youth services (Scottish Executive 2009), and as part of student evaluations of higher education (O'Neill 2015).

Figure 4.5: H-Form

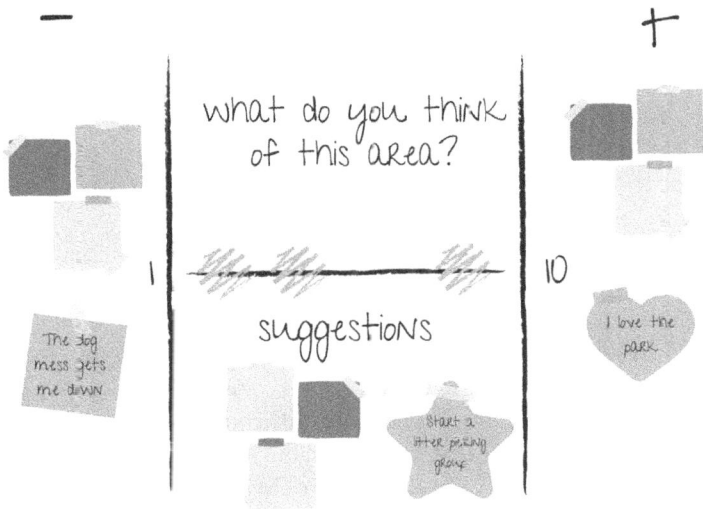

The H-Form features a continuum line at its core, which can either be employed as a standalone method or incorporated into the larger tool. This continuum line enables participants to position themselves or their viewpoints on a scale of 1–10 regarding any given topic, effectively gauging the diversity of perspectives within the group. To add an element of fun and boost energy, we often transform the continuum line into an interactive exercise, asking participants to physically stand on an imaginary line drawn across the room. This dynamic approach not only encourages active engagement but also allows individuals to explain their choices, sometimes inspiring others to reconsider their positions (Creative Facilitation 2020).

The H-Form builds on the continuum by encouraging participants to identify specific positive or negative factors influencing their position on the line. These factors can then be clustered and discussed through a facilitated process to determine necessary actions to strengthen positive factors or address negative factors in support of an overall objective. In our research projects, the use of the continuum line on the H-Form depends on the question or topic of focus, some questions being more conducive to scoring than others.

The H-Form has been proven to be an effective tool in enabling individuals and groups to document their views and ideas in a nonthreatening, open, yet structured way (Guy and Inglis 1999). It promotes individual expression as well as mutual understanding and consensus. The H-Form can be utilised in various settings, including closed group sessions as part of fieldwork and more open street-based work in public venues such as market stalls and public libraries. Its clear framework keeps discussions focused, specific, and progressive, easily leading to actionable points (Guy and Inglis 1999).

Like the graffiti wall, the H-Form can be displayed in a large format on a wall or table, allowing numerous options and suggestions to be collected in a single session. Its straightforward structure enables people to read other's comments and respond with their own thoughts and ideas without a facilitator present.

The H-Form is a versatile and valuable resource throughout the PAR process, particularly during the fieldwork stage. Its flexibility allows it to serve multiple purposes, including the following:

1. **Delving deeper into issues:** The H-Form is effective at digging into and focusing on ideas, issues or topics that emerged through other tools, ensuring a more comprehensive understanding of the topic at hand.
2. **Facilitating open discussions on new areas**: The H-Form's adaptability makes it suitable for exploring both broad and focused issues, accommodating various research 'grains'.

In the later stages of the research process, the H-Form continues to demonstrate its versatility and utility. It serves as an effective tool to:

1. **Consolidate information and provide structure:** The H-Form is particularly effective in providing a way to bring together wide-ranging and seemingly disparate data gathered through other tools. This allows the research team to identify patterns and connections, which in turn enables the group to move towards action planning in a more informed and organised manner.
2. **Facilitate analysis of existing data:** The H-Form can also be used to start the process of analysis and interpretation

of data gathered in the research room by the community researcher team. This is particularly useful partway through the fieldwork process, to help the team to identify themes, as well as under-explored areas or avenues to explore through subsequent research sessions.

The Causal Impact Diagram

The Causal Impact Diagram (see Figure 4.6) looks at the possible causes of something and the effects that it might have. It is particularly effective at identifying and understanding complex issues by breaking them down into smaller parts. Like the Spider Diagram (see Figure 4.7), the Causal Impact Diagram was developed in the 1970s and 1980s, and became part of the Rapid Rural Appraisal, Participatory Appraisal and Participatory

Figure 4.6: Causal Impact Diagram

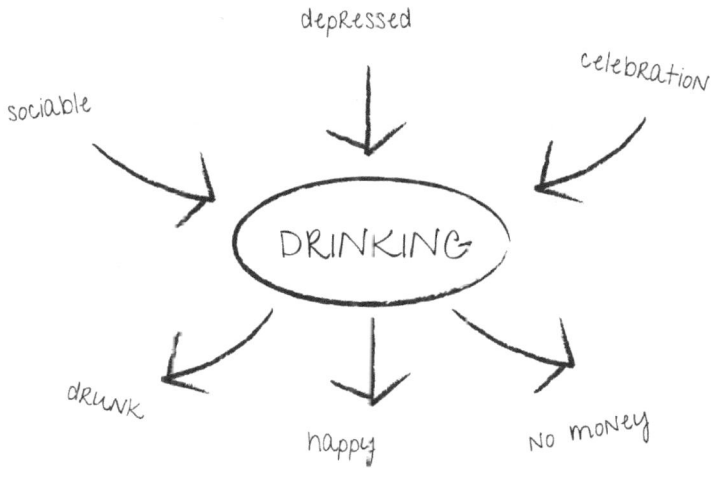

Learning and Action toolkits, in order to bring grassroots perspectives into development programmes (Pretty 1995l Shah, Kambou, and Monahan 1999; Chambers 2013).

Causal Impact Diagrams can be effectively utilised on flipcharts to facilitate group discussions and analysis. The central issue for discussion is written in the middle of the chart. Participants then identify potential causes and write them above the issue, while the impacts on individuals and the wider community are listed below.

It is important to note that some factors may act as both causes and effects. For example, poverty can limit access to quality education, while limited education can make it harder to escape poverty. Here, cause and effect reinforce one another, creating a persistent cycle. Recognising these interrelationships allows for a deeper understanding of the issue and encourages participants to explore potential solutions that could break the cycle and prevent its recurrence.

Variations of the Causal Impact Diagram include tree and fishbone diagrams. In problem tree diagrams, the central issue or topic is represented by the trunk, with different strategies or behaviours as roots and the resulting effects as branches (Kesby 2000, p 431) (Sadanandan et al 2007, p 32). Fishbone diagrams, commonly used in product design, depict the main problem or defect as the fish's head, with causes extending to the left as fishbones. The ribs represent major contributing factors, while sub-branches detail root causes, allowing for a multilevel analysis (Ishikawa 1982). Both adaptations provide a visual representation of complex issues, enabling systematic analysis and improved problem solving in a variety of sectors and settings.

Casual Impact Diagrams are particularly useful in the midst of the fieldwork stage in the following ways:

1. **Helping to explore issues in all their complexity:** In closed group sessions, Casual Impact Diagrams can really help people think through the complexities of cause and effect (for example, see Box 4.5). In health and public health contexts, these diagrams offer a comprehensive view of the complex factors influencing wellbeing, such as the impact of safety in public spaces on active lifestyles.

2. **Enabling a deeper focus to identify root causes:** Continuous exploration of cause-and-effect relationships helps reveal the deep roots of complex issues like homelessness. For instance, lack of affordable housing, caused by an imbalanced market, inadequate policies, and limited social housing funding, results in increased homelessness. Further analysis exposes poor physical and mental health outcomes as effects of homelessness, stemming from limited healthcare access, inadequate shelter, and chronic stress.

> **Box 4.5: Uncovering hidden impacts**
>
> Using the Causal Impact Diagram, a health worker brought together parents (mostly mothers) and professionals responsible for the policy of weighing children in schools and sending letters home when a child was overweight. It was widely believed by the health profession at the time that this was a key way of motivating families to eat more healthily and to take exercise. An impact diagram was used asking what mothers felt when they received the letter. The professionals were shocked at the responses: guilt, shame, embarrassment, helplessness, feeling trapped by lack of money, time and other pressures, and consequent lack of motivation.

The Spider Diagram

The Spider Diagram is an effective tool for identifying barriers and exploring potential solutions in various contexts. It has been successfully applied in participatory research projects worldwide, such as understanding obstacles and opportunities in implementing tuberculosis services in Kenya (Pola 2024), discussing research ethics with UK higher education students (Askins 2008), and addressing HIV/AIDS prevention among migrant sex workers in Cambodia (Busza and Schunter 2001).

The Spider Diagram is a flexible tool that facilitates the identification of barriers and potential solutions for various groups or individuals. To create a Spider Diagram, the topic is written at the centre of a flipchart sheet. Each 'leg' of the spider represents a particular person or group, with barriers specific to them identified along the leg. Participants can then use a different colour pen or Post-it notes to document potential solutions next to each barrier. Alternatively, the diagram can be set up with each spider leg representing a specific barrier, while solutions are noted along the legs. The Spider Diagram's strength lies in its ability to visually represent complex factors in a simple, structured manner.

Spider Diagrams are simple to use and flexible, and are useful at all stages in the research process. They can be used for the following purposes:

1. **Identifying participants:** At the beginning of the research, Spider Diagrams can help identify potential participants and anticipate barriers to their involvement, allowing community researchers to develop strategies to address these obstacles based on their own lived experience knowledge.
2. **Developing a holistic understanding of barriers:** During the research, Spider Diagrams are particularly useful in projects aiming to improve services for users. By segmenting barriers by person or type, they provide insights into the diverse challenges faced by different groups while incorporating a wide range of factors, including socioeconomic and environmental aspects. The Spider Diagram is a useful tool to dig into some of the causes and effects identified using the Causal Impact Diagram (see earlier). In the context of addressing homelessness, Spider Diagrams enable exploration of barriers faced by different groups in accessing essential services, such as healthcare. For instance, examining the barriers faced by homeless women, families, or those with mental health issues could highlight distinct challenges.
3. **Focusing on potential solutions:** In the later stages of research, Spider Diagrams are instrumental in generating and comparing potential solutions or ideas for change, and target interventions tailored to various groups' specific needs and contexts.

Figure 4.7: Spider Diagram

Tools for analysis

Tools for analysis are used to support a collaborative approach to thematic analysis, allowing community researchers to refamiliarise themselves with the data collected through the fieldwork, establish initial coding, generate themes and links, define and name themes, and then make the jump to recommendations based on the data and analysis (Braun and Clarke 2022). The tools have been influenced by approaches to analysis developed by PLA and PA practitioners who recognised that people can, with little encouragement, 'reflect, recollect, note, diagram, make lists, categorise, see connections – in short, do their own analysis and generate their own insights' (Chambers 2002, p 130). They also borrow from tools used in the service design world to make sense of data collected through user research methodologies (Martin and Hanington 2012), approaches developed by IDEO and Jonathan Ball from the consultancy Designmine (Design Council n.d.b), and the related Design Council Framework for Innovation and accompanying Methods Bank (Design Council n.d.a), as well as the Institute for Cultural Affairs' (ICA) Technology

Figure 4.8: Rose, Thorn, Bud

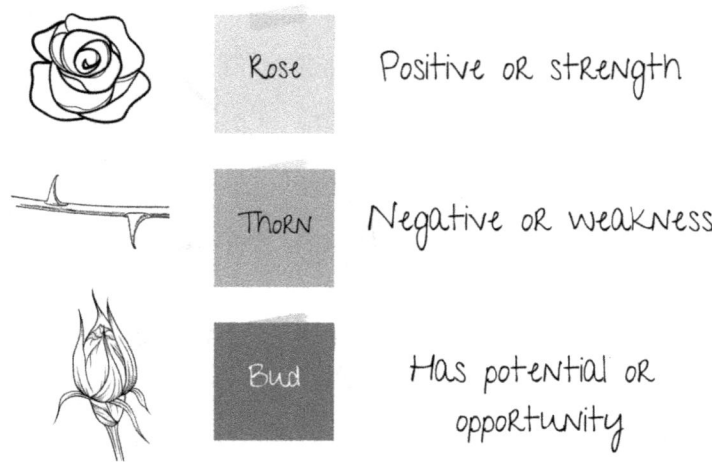

of Participation, and particularly its Consensus Workshop methodology (ICA:UK 2014).

Rose, Thorn, Bud

Rose, Thorn, Bud (see Figure 4.8) is a useful tool that supports community researchers in refamiliarising themselves with the data they have collected during fieldwork, and helps initiate the process of extrapolation and analysis by categorising data into three simple categories. Developed as part of design thinking toolkits (Crawford 2024), the method has been employed in diverse fields, including PAR projects focusing on patient-led research (Kloppenborg et al 2024), patient-centred medical communications (Starr et al 2023), and education research (Albary and Eisma 2021). To the authors' knowledge, this is the first time that the Rose, Thorn, Bud tool has been applied as part of the PAR analysis process.

The process involves community researchers reviewing the data collected on tools and observation notes from each research session. They then work together to record one issue/idea per Post-it note, using pink for positive (Rose), blue for negative (Thorn), and green for opportunities (Bud). If the same issue is repeated, a tally is added to the bottom of the Post-it notes. Each Post-it note also includes the source group or session at the bottom. All the Post-its for each session are placed in an envelope.

If ideas don't fit into these categories, these are noted separately, as are any emerging themes that are bubbling up for the research teams.

Rose, Bud, Thorn is the first stage in the analysis process, which progresses through our next tool.

Affinity Clustering

Affinity Clustering is a useful tool to gather together the data coded through the Rose, Thorn, Bud tool, compare it, and generate links and wider themes across the dataset. Also known as Affinity Diagramming, the tool is traced back to the Japanese anthropologist Jiro Kawakita and has subsequently been adapted to design thinking toolkits as a way to 'externalise and meaningfully cluster observations and insights from research, keeping design teams grounded in data as they design' (Martin and Hanington 2012, p 19; see also Beyer and Holtzblatt 1998).

Figure 4.9: Affinity Clustering

Affinity Clustering begins by gathering the envelopes containing Post-it notes from the fieldwork. The first step is to work through each envelope as a team, reviewing every Post-it note together and discussing its content to ensure a collective understanding. Working as a team, community researchers edit the notes for clarity if necessary.

As the team progresses through the data, they start identifying and grouping Post-it notes with similar themes, concepts, or ideas. These groupings will form initial clusters. These are initially organised on a flipchart using distinct icons or symbols, such as a 'fish' or 'star', to visually represent and differentiate each group. We added this stage to the process, drawing from the ICA's Consensus Workshop method (ICA:UK 2014), under the guidance of Bhavesh Patel.

Throughout the sorting process, team members are encouraged to consider various aspects to help them identify patterns and build meaningful connections within the data. These aspects may include similarities, differences, relationships, contradictions, and exceptions.

Teams should also pay attention to cluster sizes. If a cluster accumulates more than five or six Post-it notes, it is advisable to divide it into smaller, more specific groups (ICA:UK 2014). Regularly reassessing clusters and their contents is essential for maintaining a clear and concise overview of the data. It is also important to keep an open mind, as data and clusters may evolve as the analysis progresses.

Once the clusters have been defined and the teams are satisfied with their work, the naming stage begins. This involves looking at the clustered groupings and collaboratively naming each one with a specific focus on the research question or topic area under study. It is important to try and represent everything in the cluster using a descriptive name consisting of three to seven words (ICA:UK 2014). The naming process can lead to the division, combination, or re-evaluation of clusters (ICA:UK 2014). Once the names have been agreed upon, they are written on larger yellow Post-it notes to replace the icons or symbols on the flipchart.

The Rose, Thorn, Bud, and Affinity Clustering tools can be employed midway through the fieldwork period for the following purposes:

1. **To help researchers take stock of the current status of the research and identify future directions or gaps in the research:** This assists in ensuring a comprehensive understanding of the data collected and facilitates better decision making for the next steps in the research process.
2. **To familiarise researchers with the analysis process, relatively early on in the research, when there are less data to grapple with:** This allows researchers to become more adept and prepared for the final analysis workshops at the end of the fieldwork period.

These tools are also beneficial at the end of the fieldwork period for the following reasons:

1. **To help researchers integrate and make sense of the large quantity of data collected**: By using these tools, researchers can work collaboratively to organise and interpret the data effectively, as well as maintain consistency in the meaning of codes and themes across the research team.
2. **To facilitate the transition from raw data to research findings and recommendations:** Focusing on the core research theme or overarching question enables researchers to draw meaningful conclusions and develop appropriate recommendations based on the data analysis.

Tools for action planning

Transitioning from analysis tools to decision-making and action-oriented tools is crucial for implementing change based on research findings. These tools facilitate collaboration among participants, researchers, and stakeholders to collectively evaluate potential solutions, determine feasibility, and devise implementation strategies.

Ranking and scoring tools

A rich range of methods exists to enable the ranking and scoring of ideas in PAR projects. They were developed as part of PRA, PLA, and PA approaches to understand the relative importance of particular assets, or scarcity in resources or infrastructure within particular communities (Chambers 1992, p 18; Cavestro 2003, p 38). They were also used to compare preferences across different groups – for example, women and men (Chambers 1997).

The Bean Counter

The Bean Counter (see Figure 4.10) is a straightforward tool that allows participants to rank their ideas, issues, or priorities. This method is useful for identifying the most popular choices within a group. It is also easy to understand and fast to implement, enabling participants to take part with or without a facilitator present.

To implement the Bean Counter tool, ideas or issues identified earlier in the PAR process are written on a sheet of flipchart paper. Sticky dots are then made available or distributed to all participants, who are asked to allocate these dots to their top choices from the list. Once everyone has cast their votes, the most favoured choices will become apparent.

To further analyse the results, additional tools such as Impact Criteria and Impact Matrix can be employed. These tools facilitate a more comprehensive examination and evaluation of the prioritised ideas, issues, or priorities.

Figure 4.10: Bean Counter

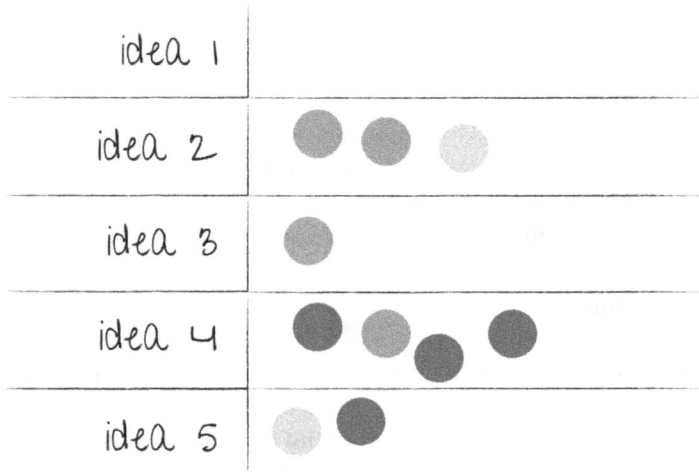

Figure 4.11: Criteria Ranking

	cost	distance	exercise
car			
bike			
bus			
train			

Criteria Ranking

Criteria Ranking (see Figure 4.11) builds on the Bean Counter by adding greater nuance to the ranking process. In order to implement Criteria Ranking, participants first organise the ideas generated from earlier research tools into the grid. Next, participants collectively determine the criteria by which all the items will be assessed, encouraging discussions to ensure that the chosen criteria are relevant and well defined.

A scoring system is then employed to evaluate each item against the established criteria. There are different methods for scoring, the most common being the allocation of a fixed number of seeds, counters, or stickers to each participant to spread across the boxes in the grid (Chambers 2002, p 137).

Once groups have ranked items, participants walk around and debate where there are differences. This may result in some changes in ranking. At the end of the process, the best option can then be determined by adding up the scores at the end of the exercise.

The Impact Matrix

The Impact Matrix (see Figure 4.12) is a valuable tool used in participatory processes to help identify and prioritise solutions

Figure 4.12: Impact Matrix

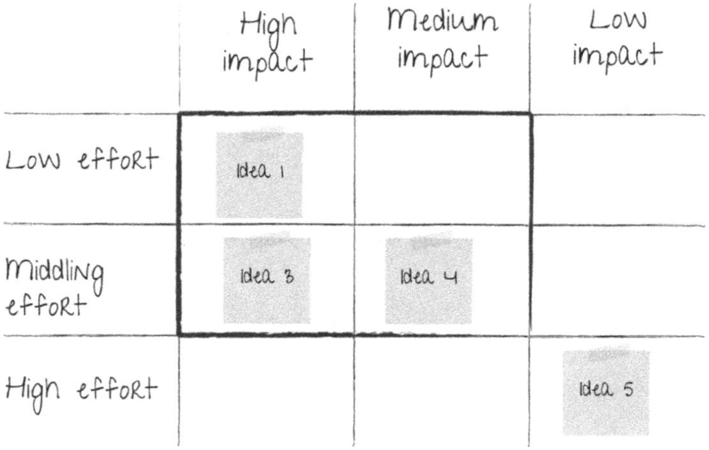

	High impact	Medium impact	Low impact
Low effort	Idea 1		
Middling effort	Idea 3	Idea 4	
High effort			Idea 5

based on their potential impact and feasibility. This tool proves particularly effective when managing a large number of proposed solutions gathered during fieldwork, as it facilitates the narrowing down and prioritisation of these ideas. By organising proposed solutions within a grid or matrix, participants can visually assess each solution's effectiveness and the ease of its implementation. This tool has been widely used in various fields, including user experience (UX) and service design (Unger and Chandler 2009), as well as management and business studies, often as part of Root Cause Analysis (Andersen and Fagerhaug 2006).

To create an Impact Matrix, a 2 x 2 grid is drawn on a large piece of paper or flipchart: the vertical axis is labelled 'Impact' (high to low) and the horizontal axis 'Feasibility' (easy to hard). Post-it notes are used to place proposed solutions within the appropriate quadrant based on their perceived impact and feasibility. Using Post-its means that the solutions can be moved if people change their minds as the discussion progresses. Whether or not a solution will be easy to implement may depend on many things, such as time, resources, and stakeholder backing/consensus. Having ranked the possible solutions, participants can then focus on those placed in the top-left-hand squares first, as these are the ones they have identified as having the greatest impact and being the easiest to implement.

Ranking and scoring tools can be used towards the end of a project to help in the following ways:

1. **Narrowing down solutions:** Towards the end of a project, ranking and scoring tools can be used to prioritise solutions gathered during the fieldwork period. By involving various perspectives, researchers can determine which ideas should be focused on, particularly when there are numerous potential solutions to consider.
2. **Progressing from idea generation to tangible solutions:** Utilising these tools in individual fieldwork sessions with closed groups enables conversations to shift from ideation to practical solutions based on an understanding of local constraints and feasibility.
3. **Empowering community researchers:** Ranking and scoring tools can help community researchers to make the jump from their research findings to concrete recommendations. This process enables community researchers to take ownership of the project and its outcomes, further strengthening their roles in the research process.
4. **Validating findings and fostering continued engagement:** These tools can be used to validate researcher findings and continue the dialogue with stakeholders and the wider community. By incorporating ranking and scoring tools in celebration and sharing events, researchers can promote transparency and collaboration throughout the research process.
5. **Fostering collaboration and accountability:** Ranking and scoring tools act as catalysts for open discussion and collaboration among diverse stakeholder groups, including community members, researchers, funders, and commissioners. When utilised in validation or celebration events, these tools facilitate conversations about actionable change, ensuring that constraints and possibilities are thoroughly understood and key stakeholders are held accountable for project outcomes

Tools for evaluation

This section introduces the tools we use to support evaluation and reflection, which are fully embedded in our PAR process and used consistently, particularly at the end of training sessions. As discussed in earlier sections, we also employ other tools, such as the timeline for reflecting on the highs and lows of a project, and the H-Form, which provides a quiet space for participants to consider how things have gone. In this section, we focus on two tools that we use regularly. We value these tools because, unlike standard feedback surveys, they allow participants to define their own evaluation criteria-identifying what is most important to them.

Evaluation Betty

Evaluation Betty (see Figure 4.13) is an adapted version of a widely used participatory feedback tool often known as *Head, Heart, Bag, Bin* (Quaker Social Action 2018; Heathcare Improvement Scotland n.d.). It was first developed in this form by Roger Newton together with community researchers working on the Joseph Rowntree Foundation's Neighbourhood Approaches to Loneliness project (JRF 2013). Within that work, Betty quickly became more than just a tool: she took on the role of

Figure 4.13: Evaluation Betty

a 'friend' to the project, supporting self-reflection, opening up conversations, and providing a nonthreatening way for participants and researchers alike to think about what they were learning. By personifying evaluation, Betty made the process feel more approachable, friendly, and engaging – in stark contrast to the dry or formal feedback methods often associated with evaluation.

We now use Betty as a light-touch evaluation method at the end of training sessions and workshops to gather quick, meaningful feedback from community researchers and participants. Unlike traditional feedback forms, which can feel formal or burdensome, Evaluation Betty provides an accessible, often playful way of reflecting that helps people feel more comfortable sharing their honest views.

To run the activity, we draw a simple figure of 'Betty' on a flipchart and introduce the four categories (Quaker Social Action 2018):

- **Head:** What have you learnt or discovered (skills, insights, or new knowledge)?
- **Heart:** What have you felt or experienced (emotions, connections, or memorable moments)?
- **Bag:** What will you take away (intentions, skills, or new practices to carry forward)?
- **Bin:** What would you throw away or change (frustrations, dislikes, or suggestions for improvement)?

Participants write their reflections on Post-it notes and place them on the relevant part of Betty. We often leave the room while the activity takes place so that participants feel free to be candid, and one of the community researchers usually facilitates the exercise, both reinforcing our 'participatory from the start' ethos and offering them the opportunity to build facilitation skills.

Evaluation Betty has many variations, sometimes appearing as *Evaluation Bob* or being themed to suit a project. For example, physiotherapist Clare McCarroll adapted the tool as *Evaluation Freddie* (after Fred Astaire) to gather feedback on dance-based physiotherapy sessions for people with dementia (see McCarroll's work with the Brain Charity: Brain Charity n.d). What makes Betty particularly powerful is its accessibility: because it doesn't depend heavily on literacy, it creates a more open and gentle space

Figure 4.14: Pizza Pie

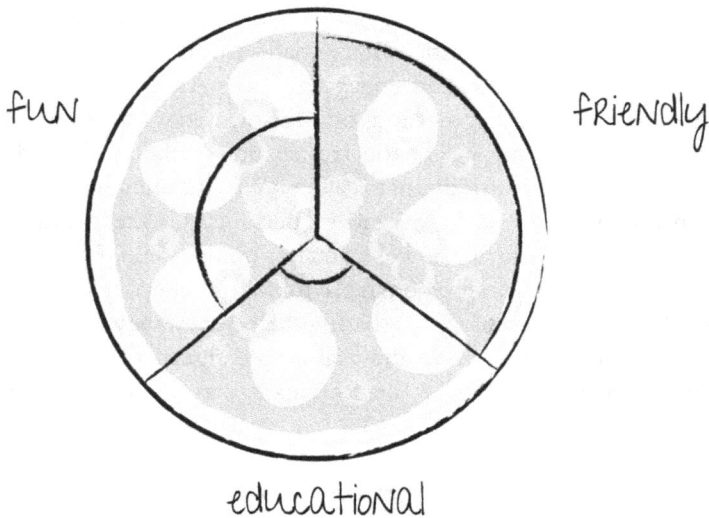

for feedback, making it especially suitable for participants with neurodiversity or cognitive differences. The humour and creativity behind these adaptations also help to reduce barriers, making the tool engaging and highly flexible across contexts.

The Evaluation Wheel (Pizza Pie)

The Evaluation Wheel, sometimes nicknamed the 'Pizza Pie', is a participatory tool for assessing whether an activity, event, or project is meeting the needs of participants. Evaluation Wheels in various guises are widely used in evaluation processes (Evaluation Support Scotland 2019). We build on these foundations, but instead of predefining the criteria to be scored, we invite participants themselves to define the criteria that matter most to them (Sport England n.d.).

To use the tool, a circle is divided into segments, with each segment representing one of the criteria chosen by participants – for example, how fun, friendly, welcoming, or educational an event felt. Each criterion is scored from 0 to 10, with the segment shaded in accordingly: if the score is 1, only a tenth of the segment is filled; if it is 10, the whole segment is coloured. Once the wheel is complete, the group can easily see whether their expectations were met, and in what areas improvements might be needed.

The real value of the Evaluation Wheel lies not in the final scores, but in the conversations that happen around them. Discussing why something was scored highly – or why it fell short – provides important insights into what participants value most and what changes could make the experience stronger. In this way, the tool is both visual and dialogic, creating an accessible, engaging process of collective reflection.

A version of the wheel can also be used to support individual self-reflection. For example, community researchers in training might plot their skills, knowledge, and confidence across different areas, scoring themselves at the start and end of the process. This helps them identify personal strengths, track progress, and highlight where they want to focus future development or support.

Conclusions

In conclusion, we have presented a selection of tools in this chapter that we have found to be beneficial in our PAR projects. While this list is not exhaustive, we hope that it serves as a useful starting point for others and inspires further exploration. As mentioned at the beginning of this chapter, these tools alone cannot accomplish the objectives of PAR, but they do provide a solid foundation for promoting dialogue, encouraging diverse perspectives, and fostering understanding. Their appeal lies in their ability to facilitate conversations that are less confrontational and intimidating, as they invite participants to gather around, to look at issues from a different perspective, and to be creative. We wholeheartedly encourage you to try these tools for yourselves, as the best way to learn is through hands-on experience. Embrace the process – and happy researching!

5

Reflections on ethics and power

PAR is an approach that stands out for its commitment to ethical practices and its dedication to acknowledging, questioning, and subverting power structures (Freire 2017). PAR carries a radical intent that aims to disrupt existing hierarchies and empower marginalised communities. This spirit of challenging the status quo is a thread that has persisted throughout the evolution of PAR over many years.

In this chapter, we explore the various ways power dynamics can be disrupted at the micro-level through PAR projects, with a particular focus on amplifying the voices of marginalised groups in society. These groups include women, working-class people, refugees, disabled people, and LGBTQ+ communities and minority communities, who face systemic barriers and discrimination. Our focus is on addressing power imbalances within the everyday interactions between professionals, managers, and people with less power, including workers lower down the hierarchy, users of public services, and community members. We recognise that PAR cannot single-handedly dismantle systemic inequities, but we argue that it can be instrumental in fostering more equitable relationships between commissioning clients and professional stakeholders, facilitator trainers, community researchers, and research participants.

Drawing on the early practitioners of PRA and PLA, we emphasise the importance of valuing lived experience and local knowledge as much as expert knowledge. By doing so, PAR seeks to break down the distance between professionals, expert researchers, and local people, ultimately 'handing over the stick' – both literally and metaphorically – to transfer authority and initiative (Chambers 2002, p 3).

After a discussion of research ethics in PAR, we present 13 ways in which we and others have stumbled in our projects, alongside 13 strategies for countering these pitfalls. Inspired by Robert Chambers' *A Sourcebook of Ideas and Activities for Participatory Workshops*, we pick up his invitation for readers to reflect on their own experiences and create their own lists (2002, p 13). Through this approach, we hope to contribute to the ongoing conversation about the importance of challenging power dynamics, which we see as being at the heart of ethical research practice, and fostering more equitable collaborations in PAR.

Research ethics and Participatory Action Research

PAR projects do not always fit easily within conventional ethical processes, and often lack access to formal ethics committees such as those available in universities. Even when formal reviews are possible, they can be ill-suited to the realities of PAR. Because PAR seeks to involve people from the very beginning of a project, before research questions, methods, or fieldwork plans are fully defined, it can be difficult to meet review processes that demand a fixed rationale and a detailed outline of all potential risks and procedures in advance (Kara 2018). Another limitation is that most ethics committees do not include representatives of the communities who are being researched or community researchers themselves, raising questions about whose perspectives count (Kara 2018). Requirements such as lengthy consent forms may also create barriers for projects working with marginalised or overpoliced groups, where bureaucratic processes can heighten anxiety and fuel distrust in research (Kara 2018). In response to these limitations, some scholars and practitioners have sought to reimagine ethical review as a more collaborative and flexible process, leading to the development of shared standards and frameworks tailored to the values of PAR.

One way of addressing these challenges has been through the development of shared ethical standards for PAR, both inside and outside academia. The *Centre for Social Justice and Community Action* and the *National Coordinating Centre for Public Engagement* (2012) developed a framework that foregrounds values such as mutual respect, equality and inclusion, democratic participation, active learning, collective action, and personal integrity. Their guide also offers practical prompts for researchers and community partners to reflect on together: why they are working in partnership, who should be involved and with what responsibilities, how sensitive information will be managed, how findings will be shared and credited, what kinds of change they are aiming for, and what a 'good ending' to the work might look like. These questions encourage ethics to be seen not as a hurdle to overcome at the outset, but as an ongoing, practical concern.

Outside academia, Participatory Practitioners for Change (Rowley, Doyle, and Hay 2013) developed ethical standards specifically for community contexts. Their framework combined broad principles of PAR with practical guidance for commissioners and promises for practitioners. The commissioner guidance is particularly valuable, stressing the importance of flexibility, openness to unexpected findings, feeding back to participants, and ensuring that projects genuinely promote action and capacity building. Their practitioner promises include the need to clarify roles, communicate findings in a timely way, build long-term capacity, include diverse participants, ensure informed consent, and faithfully report findings even when they are challenging to stakeholders. More recently, the Young Foundation's Principles of Peer Research (2024b) emphasise reciprocity, care, and ethical rigour. Peer researchers should receive proper training, recognition, and compensation, while professional researchers should remain open to being challenged and learning from lived experience. Together, these frameworks frame ethics as a shared responsibility rather than a set of external requirements to comply with.

Banks and Brydon-Miller (2018) extend this perspective by showing how ethics in PAR is less about fixed rules and more about relationships. They emphasise the idea of 'everyday ethics', where ethical practice is woven into daily decisions, interactions, and reflections. This concept has also been applied in other forms of qualitative research, including non-participatory approaches, as a way to challenge the 'tick-box' or overly narrow procedures of some ethics committees, and to underline the ongoing and evolving moral challenges involved in researching with people (Rossman and Rallis 2010). These issues are especially pronounced in PAR, which requires extending traditional or procedural views of ethics, which focus on confidentiality, consent, and protection of 'subjects', to encompass more fluid and complex questions about partnership, shared power, evolving research agendas, and the personal and emotional impacts of collaboration and disclosure. Banks and colleagues (2013) describe the 'messiness' of ethics in practice: the difficulties of gaining consent in changing circumstances, the emotional burden carried by both researchers and participants, and the risks of powerful stakeholders dismissing or undermining lived experience. Their work reminds us that ethics in PAR is not a one-off requirement, but an ongoing negotiation shaped by trust, sensitivity, and care.

Questions of vulnerability add another layer of complexity. As Aldridge (2016) argues, even the label of 'vulnerable' is problematic, particularly when it results in excluding people from participation in research. Vulnerability is not a neutral category but a contested one, shaped by the perspectives of those 'doing the defining' rather than by any inherent qualities of participants (2016, p 1). Ryan's (2019) work on disability and austerity underscores this point, showing how structural inequalities and policy decisions create vulnerability rather than it being a fixed characteristic of individuals. In this context, Aldridge emphasises that research projects and methods must be designed to actively counter feelings of powerlessness among marginalised people, avoiding the reinforcement of vulnerability or the risk of further harm. Her work with women survivors of domestic violence demonstrates how storytelling approaches can enable participants to reclaim their narratives and strengthen their sense of being believed – a vital step in recovery. Likewise, her research with young people and those with profound learning difficulties, who would be unlikely to thrive in traditional research contexts that rely heavily on abstract reasoning, memory, and verbal contributions (Aldridge 2016, p 3), highlights the importance of participatory visual methods in enabling meaningful involvement. These ways of working exemplify how research can affirm participants' competence and agency, showing that ethics in

PAR is not a matter of tick-box compliance, but something fundamentally embedded in the design and practice of the research itself.

Taking these debates further, Helen Kara (2018) invites Euro-Western researchers to learn from Indigenous research ethics. She cautions that not all Indigenous researchers follow the same ethical principles, but as a student of the Indigenous research paradigm, she identifies four key ones. The first is *relational accountability*: researchers have long-term accountability to those with whom they are in relationship, including both human and nonhuman beings. This involves continually asking how research can help maintain and strengthen the relationships on which it is built. Building on the work of Weber-Pillwax (2001) and Chilisa (2012, p 118), Kara stresses that researchers need to consider very carefully how the methods they choose can build respectful relationships – between the topic of study and the research, the research and the researcher, and crucially, between the researcher and participants (Kara 2018, p 26). The second principle is the *community of knowledge*, which recognises that everyone has valuable knowledge to contribute and that knowledge itself cannot be 'owned'. Rather, knowledge is shared and collectively held, belonging to everyone – not just in the present moment but across time and space. The third is *reciprocity*, which emphasises that relationships must be mutual – between people, but also between researchers and the environment. This means never taking more than is needed, and centring care and respect for both human communities and the natural world (2018, p 26). The fourth is *benefit sharing*, which insists that participants and communities should benefit from research as much as researchers do. This requires co-defining research questions and investigations in order to understand what communities want, and what they would find useful (2018, p 27). These principles contrast sharply with the Euro-Western approach to ethics, which, as Kara argues, often focuses inward – on the processes of the research project itself – rather than outward, on the impact research could have on structural inequalities (2018, p 3). This perspective underscores that the research process as a whole should be oriented towards making positive change, addressing power both in process and in purpose.

This brings us to the question of who controls the ethics or ethical foundations of a research project, and whether these should be externally judged. In our view, ethics are deeply embedded in our work – they cannot simply be imposed from the outside. Everyone brings their own values and ethical perspectives, which shape the way they work, making open discussion essential. During our community research training, we spend a substantial amount of time talking about ethics and co-defining an ethical framework for each project. As Box 5,1 shows, ethical practice is something we both codify and 'teach' to community researchers, but it is always defined collaboratively, reflecting our shared responsibility and values.

> **Box 5.1: Community researcher-led ethics**
>
> Two of our community researchers, Sohrab Rezvani and Liz Duffy, worked together to define a set of ethics as a foundation for a project exploring social tenant experiences of low-energy retrofit improvements to their homes.
>
> *Baseline ethical terms of engagement*:
>
> - Clearly communicate the research purpose and intended use of participants' input.
> - Ensure participants understand their involvement is voluntary and they don't have to take part.
> - Avoid pressuring or probing for information without consent.
> - Strive for anonymity and avoid collecting personally identifiable data.
> - Maintain a feedback loop for transparency.
>
> *Agency and ownership over the research*:
>
> - Offer participants opportunities to continue their involvement in the research and wider project.
> - Provide space for them to define new directions in the research.

Take care of everybody's needs:

- Being in a neutral space so that people are happy to say what they feel.
- Provide a comfortable environment, with nice food and drink.
- Accommodate preferences for one-on-one or small group interactions.
- Ensure accessibility needs are addressed, including language and disability considerations.
- Restrict any oppressive or abusive language.

Holding the space for people:

- Adopt an attentive, empathetic attitude towards participants' feelings.
- Provide a safe space for them to share without judgement.

Provide help, support, and actionable knowledge:

- Actively facilitate shared learning and support between participants.
- Refer them to additional resources.
- Offer opportunities to learn more about retrofitting and practical ways to improve their homes.

There are two key takeaways from this discussion on ethics and PAR. First, ethics is not a one-off moment at the start of a research project; it is something that lives and breathes throughout the work, as ethical dilemmas and difficulties arise continuously. Second, these dilemmas are more often than not about power. Social justice is inherently political, and politics is ultimately about power. For us, ethical practice means identifying, revealing, and seeking to rebalance power – a theme explored further in the pitfalls and solutions discussed in the remainder of this chapter.

Thirteen pitfalls in challenging power in Participatory Action Research and 13 ideas to overcome them

Pitfall 1: overly restrictive research questions

Professionals, including commissioners and project managers, may be inclined to define research questions too narrowly due to a fear of letting go, a lack of trust in the process and techniques of PAR, and the pressure to deliver results within the context of demanding jobs, organisational targets, and funding restrictions/ requirements. This approach can limit the scope of the research, preventing community researchers and participants from exploring topics and questions that are meaningful to them. Often, this is based on a lack of understanding of PAR and greater familiarity and trust in more conventional research methods with more closely defined research questions, such as surveys, structured interviews, and focus groups. Defining research questions is ultimately a question of power, as it involves deciding what is important and what should be excluded from the research project. When professionals cannot hand over this power and enable community researchers to define and refine questions in the process of conducting their research, the research process becomes less engaging, more frustrating, and less empowering.

Solution: empowering collaborative question development

PAR, at its core, should be about providing a research project with the necessary scope, space, and flexibility to enable community researchers, trainer-facilitators, and commissioners to collaboratively identify important questions, explore wider influencing factors, and determine the best-suited solutions. While it is crucial to have a broad topic area as a starting point in the commissioner's brief, the process of refining research questions in PAR should be an iterative one, involving the testing, refining, and narrowing of questions as the project evolves.

Pitfall 2: professional power and gatekeeping

Professionals can be powerful gatekeepers who determine who participates and whose voices are considered relevant in the research. For example, we have encountered professionals who classify individuals with lived experience as 'inappropriate people', such as drug service users or those who have experienced homelessness. Unhappiness may also arise when less powerful individuals are engaged in the project and given a voice – for example, receptionists versus doctors. Others can act as gatekeepers and often speak for 'vulnerable' groups, including disabled people, children, and young people.

Solution: amplifying marginalised voices and empowering community researchers

The community researcher model is a powerful way to enable embedded community researchers to act as conduits and gatekeepers. They bring invaluable connections, define who they want to engage with, and justify their choices. In these ways, just as research questions aren't predefined, neither are research participants. When executed successfully, we build on researchers' own expertise and knowledge by recruiting a mixed team with diverse community 'ins'. This approach not only empowers community researchers but also enhances the research process by incorporating a rich variety of perspectives and experiences that we wouldn't be able to access via 'professional' links alone. Community researchers with diverse needs have been trained to take the lead and go out and speak to people from their communities. While safeguarding is crucial, it is essential to find ways to empower and amplify the voices of those who are often spoken for. This approach should be guided by an ethic of 'they can do it!' which challenges a paternalistic or patronising view of what people are capable of and what they have to offer.

Pitfall 3: rushing the research process and packing the agenda

It is common not to allocate sufficient time for a PAR project to reach its full potential. Time is often constrained by external factors, such as budgetary limitations, most notably the pressure to utilise remaining funds before the end of the fiscal year. A PAR project that is short on time often results in a poor process and, in all likelihood, a suboptimal outcome. Even if an official report is produced and proves to be useful, it is likely that the valuable skills and relationship-building benefits typically gained from the PAR process are lost.

In the training room, we as PAR practitioners can become preoccupied with covering all the training content rather than giving each activity the necessary space and time it deserves. This can lead to fatigue for both trainers and community researchers. In turn, this results in shortened breaks, extended session times, and a sense of lost control or floundering, which generates a feeling of unease and lack of confidence within the group.

As illustrated in Box 5.2, during participatory workshops professionals in the room can be fixated on getting through agenda items rather than really listening and giving space to particular conversations and tools. This can result in shutting discussions down, just when they are getting going, and can undermine trust among participants who may feel they have not been listened to.

Box 5.2: 'Feeling at home' – opening conversations on refugee women's access to healthcare in the UK

In one participatory workshop exploring the experiences of women refugees, a community researcher began by co-defining 'house rules' with the group. She explained that the goal was to create an environment where everyone felt at home, and invited participants to share what would make them comfortable and how the session could best support them. This simple act sparked a rich and open discussion: the women began sharing their experiences of accessing healthcare in the UK, and the conversation flowed naturally.

However, the project manager on the client side grew concerned that not all agenda items were being covered. They repeatedly interrupted to speak to the PAR practitioners (trainers), which disrupted the session. What they did not recognise was that the purpose of the workshop was not to tick off agenda items, but to create space for conversations to emerge and deepen.

In later workshops, we decided not to provide the agenda upfront, keeping it to ourselves instead. This gave us the

> flexibility to adapt in the moment, prioritising the flow of discussion and participant engagement over rigid adherence to pre-set items.

Solution: give it time, be flexible and prioritise community voices

To maintain the quality and impact of our work, we no longer accept projects with insufficient time allocation. We work with commissioners to ensure that project plans allow for adequate time to think, reflect, and adapt to changing circumstances.

When conducting training, it is crucial to allocate more time to each activity than you initially anticipate. Build in contingency plans from the outset – expect participants to arrive late or for unexpected interruptions to occur. Inquire about participants' preferences for breaks, including their desired frequency and duration, and make an effort to accommodate their needs. Pay close attention to the group dynamics and be flexible in adjusting the schedule as necessary. Aim to conclude the training earlier than the scheduled end time, thereby providing participants with 'bonus' additional time.

During fieldwork sessions, it is crucial to strike a balance between following a structured plan and remaining flexible enough to adapt to the groups' needs and interests. This requires a keen ability to gauge the atmosphere in the room, allowing fruitful and relevant conversations to flourish instead of cutting them off to strictly follow our initial plans. This heightened attentiveness does not indicate a lack of focus; on the contrary, it demonstrates a commitment to actively listening and prioritising participant concerns. By fostering such open and responsive communication, we can avoid overlooking or dismissing discussions that the community deems important in favour of our own predetermined judgments.

Pitfall 4: holding on to symbols of status and power

Professionals may inadvertently reinforce power imbalances by using symbols that highlight their status or institutional affiliation. For example, wearing job titles on lanyards or introducing themselves with their professional titles can create a sense of hierarchy and distance between professionals in the room and community members. At best, this practice can hinder the development of trust and rapport, which are essential for successful projects. As Box 5.3 illustrations, at worst, it can actively discourage participation among community researchers.

In addition, conventional professional practices such as PowerPoint presentations can inadvertently perpetuate a power imbalance. While these presentations are commonplace in many work environments, they can create a 'lecture-like' atmosphere that separates 'teachers' from 'learners'.

> **Box 5.3: 'Feeling left out' – how professional symbols can undermine participation**
>
> In one user-led PAR project exploring dual diagnosis (drug use and mental health issues), community researchers – all with lived experience of dual diagnosis – were called to a meeting with the project sponsors, an academic institution. During the meeting, each person was asked to introduce themself. Many attendees had academic or other professional roles, while one community researcher had none. This researcher felt excluded and left out, which damaged his confidence and ultimately led him to withdraw from the project.

Solution: connecting on a personal level

To mitigate the influence of power dynamics, prioritise personal connections over professional status. Recognise that individuals may feel anxious when introducing themselves in a room filled with unfamiliar people, particularly in spaces where power dynamics are at play. To alleviate this discomfort, avoid formal introductions based on professional titles and focus on getting to know one another through shared interests, experiences, or hobbies.

Icebreakers, as discussed in Chapter 3, can be a great way to help participants get to know one another without the pressure of formal introductions. Additionally, consider incorporating light-touch activities such as taking a walk or touring the project site, which can provide opportunities for informal conversations between participants. Encourage everyone to engage in chats with others one to one during these activities. Getting stuck into nonthreatening pair and small group work early on is a great way to start the process of getting to know each other.

Instead of reaching for a PowerPoint, we avoid them at all costs during training and fieldwork situations. When we do talk from the front, we try to keep it short, practical, and linked to our experiences rather than imparting knowledge in the abstract. Instead of PowerPoint, we 'de-centre' presentations by sticking up the tools we have worked on during the training all around the room (Chambers 2002). We also work hard to show that we are learning too, sitting down with the group and mucking in to help rather than elevating ourselves.

Pitfall 5: inadequate structure or support

Handing over control might sound a bit like anarchy! However, it's important to understand that this is not the case – you cannot hand over the stick without providing the support needed to hold and wield it. Sometimes clients do not want to invest the time and resources necessary for community researchers to learn and practise the tools and techniques so that they feel confident to use them, and have the time to form appropriately as a cohesive and supportive team. Without appropriate support, community researchers may feel abandoned, scared, or disempowered, and are more likely to disengage or drop out.

Solution: structured empowerment and supportive culture

To address this pitfall, we focus on key aspects that promote a more balanced and supportive environment. We begin by providing a thorough explanation of the overall PAR process at the outset, ensuring that everyone understands the goals, expectations, and potential challenges.

Investing considerable time and effort in teaching the necessary tools and techniques, we offer practical learning experiences to build confidence and competence. This includes hands-on learning in the training room, alongside supported research sessions in the community. We have also in recent years invested more in supporting logistics and facilitation where it is needed, as community researchers embark on their fieldwork. This enables community researchers to develop their skills and grow in confidence, and provides a more solid foundation for them to take the lead.

Pitfall 6: seeking perfectionism

A culture of striving for perfectionism can hinder the PAR process. This can manifest as an environment where participants are discouraged from expressing uncertainty, asking questions, admitting mistakes, or acknowledging imperfections. Such an environment can inhibit growth, learning, and genuine collaboration.

Solution: modelling imperfection and encouraging reflection

We try to give people the structure to succeed *and* fail well. We model imperfection (sometimes this is easy!) and create a more open, inclusive, and reflective atmosphere. We openly admit when we have made mistakes and use these instances as opportunities for learning and growth, helping normalise the idea that mistakes are a natural part of the process and encouraging participants to do the same. We achieve this through the use of evaluation tools which help us adapt our training sessions in response to feedback. We also encourage community researchers to do the same, through the use of reflective tools like observations and the timeline, so that we can all learn from what worked and what didn't go so well during the training, fieldwork, and analysis.

Pitfall 7: allowing people to dominate and sabotage

Facilitators often encounter individuals who dominate discussions or try to divert the group's focus. In quieter groups where participants are less forthcoming, a dominator can appear to be a valuable contributor (Chambers 2002). However, their disproportionate influence can silence quieter members, create frustration among participants, and hinder the overall progress of the group work. Dominators may include leaders, individuals with power or status, or people with personal agendas.

Solution: managing dominators and supporting quiet people to have a voice

Solutions for managing dominators and potential saboteurs involve setting ground rules that promote equal participation and encourage those who tend to dominate conversations to make space for others, and quieter members to step forward. Acknowledging the contributions of dominators and then redirecting discussions ensures that those who have not yet shared their thoughts have the opportunity to do so. We also incorporate space for individual reflection, pair work, and small group activities to create different opportunities to take part depending on preference. This helps less vocal participants to contribute in comfort and is also an essential way to cater to individuals with neurodiversities. Such participants may require a quieter space for contribution and might need more time for individual reflection before sharing their ideas and thoughts.

Pitfall 8: hoarding data and insights

It is common to operate in an extractive mode, where data are collected and researchers depart without fostering adequate dialogue or feedback on findings and recommendations. This issue persists in both PAR and conventional projects. Traditionally, we've gathered data, compiled reports, and provided insufficient opportunities for participants to engage with the research outcomes. This undermines the PAR ethos and ethical stance. Without promoting greater involvement in data sharing, analysis, and shaping outputs, the purpose of this collaborative approach becomes hollow.

Solution: enhancing collaboration and information sharing

To overcome the pitfalls of hoarding information, fostering collaboration at every stage of the research process is essential. This includes empowering community researchers to take the lead in data analysis, definition of findings, and recommendations. Opening up the writing process as a collaborative endeavour is also an important way of doing this, as is ensuring any reports are clearly co-authored. By utilising the team's knowledge and skills, findings can be shared through the most appropriate means. These include the use of creative sharing methods such as songs, drama, arts activities, and celebration events (Kara 2018, p 139). These methods can help disseminate information more broadly among project participants, stakeholders, and the wider community. Furthermore, facilitating ongoing discussions through action-focused tools can encourage engagement and maintain the collaborative spirit of the PAR approach.

Pitfall 9: professionals who 'already know it all'

Professionals may inadvertently (or overtly!) undermine the PAR process by maintaining an attitude of superiority or disregarding the value of community researchers' contributions. This can manifest in various ways, such as professionals assuming they 'already know it all', refusing to take part in participatory workshops, or becoming distracted by other priorities. During training sessions, professionals may elevate themselves and not participate fully, based on the assumption that they already know how to undertake PAR. In fieldwork or feedback sessions, professionals may not show up at all or may attend but remain distracted, such as being preoccupied with their phones or other tasks. Without prior briefing, professionals can feel under attack or believe that community researchers do not fully understand the constraints under which they work.

Solution: active support of stakeholder relationships

To address this pitfall, we implement several strategies. First, we prefer not to include workers alongside community researchers in training sessions, as this can impact the dynamics and power balance. Separate training allows community researchers to express their thoughts and opinions freely. Second, we ensure that professionals understand the scope, ethos, and values of the PAR approach by providing clear briefings. This helps them recognise the importance of community researchers' roles and the value of their contributions. Third, we facilitate engagement between community researchers and professionals through carefully briefed sessions where they can discuss their respective realities. Fourth, we manage the sharing of findings and recommendations with our clients, presenting them in a constructive manner to encourage positive and practical discussions. Lastly, we actively support community researchers by managing professional engagement and acting as mediators and advocates for their interests.

Pitfall 10: nothing changes

A significant challenge in PAR is when the collaborative efforts and research findings fail to bring about tangible change in the community or stakeholders involved. This pitfall occurs when there is a lack of follow-through on the findings and recommendations, resulting in a disconnect between the research process and real-world impact. The process can become a mere exercise in data collection and discussion without translating into meaningful action.

Solution: fostering accountability

To avoid the pitfall of a lack of tangible impact, establishing clear goals and expectations from the outset is crucial. This ensures that all parties are committed to implementing the research findings, particularly those with the power and resources to do so. Additionally, research reports should include a section outlining clients' plans for implementing actions and when they intend to do so.

Incorporating an overall project evaluation will help monitor whether targets are being acted upon and their impact measured. Linking the PAR to broader work that can be influenced at various levels, such as strategic, programme-level, or project-specific plans, will further support change implementation.

Pitfall 11: problems with pay and remuneration

Some clients and professionals fail to pay community researchers fairly for their work, overlooking the value of local expertise, and justifying it on the basis that payment may be a form of coercion, potentially influencing participants to engage in the research process due to financial incentives rather than genuine interest or commitment to the project.

> **Box 5.4: Valuing local expertise – lessons from the Single Regeneration Budget era**
>
> During the Single Regeneration Budget (SRB) in the 1990s, urban regeneration companies set rates for accounting 'in-kind' time. Typically, the contributions of professionals – such as accountants or lawyers – were valued much higher than those of local people participating in boards, committees, area reference groups, or doing actual community work.
>
> The Community Development Company successfully challenged this practice, persuading decision makers to value the contributions of local people, including those involved in PAR training and projects, at the same rate as the 'higher-ups'. This recognition acknowledged the expertise, labour, and commitment of community participants as equally important to professional input.

Too often, complicated payment processes and excessive bureaucracy can hinder timely payment and burden community researchers with tedious administrative tasks. Very often digital forms are unsuitable for community researchers who do not have access to a computer or laptop. When payment is introduced, there may be a shift in the perception of project ownership, with commissioners potentially feeling entitled to control the process and community researchers feeling like hired help rather than equal partners, with an expectation that 'employees' must follow directives without question.

Solution: pay fairly and swiftly

One simple way to avoid this pitfall is to offer community researchers fair and timely payment for their efforts, treating them as essential members of the research team to foster an atmosphere of equity and respect. Minimise bureaucratic hurdles to ensure that community researchers are paid swiftly and without undue burden, treating them with the same consideration you would expect for yourself as a freelance professional. Create an environment where trust is the foundation of collaboration, emphasising that projects belong to the entire group and encouraging shared decision making and open communication. Challenge the attitude that people with lived experience shouldn't be paid for their expertise – if everyone else in the room is being paid, why not them? (Box 5.4 shows how policies can be changed when challenged to ensure fair renumeration.) Arguably, we are all coerced into work that is paid so that we can live. In cases where direct payment may not be suitable – for example, if it could interfere with benefits eligibility – consult with community researchers about what they would value instead, such as a reference, a training course, or payment in kind.

Pitfall 12: discontinuity of Participatory Action Research projects

PAR is often commissioned on a project-by-project basis. This can result in a new set of community researchers being trained for each project, only to be released once the project concludes. Small organisations supporting community researchers' training are particularly affected by this issue, as they depend on project-based funding and commissions. This pitfall often leads to a lack of follow-up opportunities, loss of capacity, and erosion of knowledge held by community researchers and commissioning organisations.

Solutions: generating follow-up opportunities

To tackle the issue of discontinuity, developing long-term strategies and partnerships is crucial. These strategies should focus on maintaining a pool of experienced community researchers, promoting collaboration, and ensuring continuous engagement. Encouraging client organisations to integrate PAR approaches into their ongoing work can lead to sustained engagement with communities and researchers. Another solution involves creating pathways into community engagement roles within client organisations. As Box 5.5 shows, providing follow-up opportunities to get involved as trainers is also a good way to build skills and capacity of community researchers, as is opening up opportunities to work on other projects when the fit is right.

> **Box 5.5: From community researchers to Participatory Action Research trainers**
>
> As part of a PAR training course for academics at John Moores University, we invited a team of community researchers we had previously worked with to join us as co-trainers. They were paid a professional rate for their role and took the lead in several sessions, including discussions on research ethics, reflections on the highs and lows of being a community researcher, and strategies for sharing findings in ways that are accessible to diverse audiences. Their contributions brought enormous value to the learner group, offering first-hand accounts of working on a live PAR project. At the same time, the process created opportunities for the community researchers to share their expertise, strengthen their skills, and provide practical, actionable advice to others at the beginning of their own PAR journeys.

Pitfall 13: failing to protect trainer/facilitator wellbeing

In PAR projects, while safeguarding and supporting community researchers and participants are quite rightly prioritised, the wellbeing of practitioners may be overlooked. As Kara (2018, pp 161–162) points out, there are few ethical guidelines that mention researcher wellbeing and when they do, they tend to focus on physical safety rather than emotional risks of difficult subject matter, lack of support, and isolation, conflict, and stress.

PAR projects are often demanding and unpredictable: they require flexibility and responsiveness, which can be challenging to manage. The political complexity of managing expectations and navigating relationships with clients and other stakeholders can also contribute to stress. Managing a team of community researchers and ensuring that everyone feels valued can feel like a lot to carry. Simultaneously handling logistics, fieldwork support, payments, expenses, client relationships, the development of creative outputs, and event planning can be overwhelming. Practitioners are also often managing multiple projects at one time. All these factors can lead to burnout.

Additionally, low contract values and poor compensation can affect freelancers' and independents' ability to plan for their future, save for pensions, or prepare for periods of ill health.

Solutions: supporting trainer/facilitator wellbeing

Supporting the wellbeing of trainers and facilitators in PAR projects requires careful attention to the relationships and environments in which they work. One essential aspect is fostering a supportive team environment that includes the client, the community researchers, and fellow practitioners. Investing time in client briefing and clearly defining roles and responsibilities helps avoid difficulties in practitioner–client relationships. A supportive client can make an enormous difference, creating a sense of safety for everyone involved.

Equally important is investing in the community researcher team and seeing oneself as part of that team. As Box 5.6 shows, PAR facilitators not only support community researchers – they also receive support in return. This reciprocity is central to the power balancing we strive for in PAR: while PAR facilitators take on additional responsibilities, we are also human, and solidarity within the team matters.

> **Box 5.6: Small acts of care**
>
> After one analysis day with a team of community researchers evaluating a localised public health campaign on gynaecological cancers, the group realised that the PAR facilitator had a long journey home, late at night. Concerned for their wellbeing, the researchers quietly put together a box of treats to keep the facilitator going on the

> way back. This small act of care is just one example of how, in PAR, support flows both ways, reminding us that we are not only colleagues but also human beings who look out for each other.

As explored in Chapter 3, we advocate for teams of three community researchers on our PAR projects. This is crucial for ensuring physical safety, emotional wellbeing, and mutual support during fieldwork. In our experience, a three-person team on the trainer/facilitator side is also optimal: one person focuses on overall project management and coordination, another serves as a co-trainer to support training and delivery, and a third provides fieldwork support, managing logistics, attending sessions, and troubleshooting as needed. This collaborative structure not only ensures the necessary support for community researchers, but also helps distribute the workload and responsibilities involved in delivering the projects effectively.

In addition to a supportive team environment, advocating for better pay and conditions is vital. As Kara and Baines (2023) argue, independent social researchers are at a disadvantage in accessing public funding to support their research, and face challenges including financial precarity. This is an equity issue, with many going it alone, motivated by the need to balance their careers with caring roles (Hay and Harness 2015). Although addressing structural issues around pay and conditions can be challenging, it is essential for PAR practitioners who work as independents to understand the value of their work, quote projects appropriately, and effectively communicate the social impact and value of the PAR approach. Upskilling in running a freelance or small business with a social focus is crucial – for example. through structured programmes like those run by the School of Social Entrepreneurs (School for Social Entrepreneurs n.d.). The UK Forum for Independent Researchers has also recently published a useful free downloadable guide for independent scholars (Haste and Baines 2024).

New initiatives, including the recently established Mighty Mini Research Collective (Mighty Mini Research Collective n.d.; see Box 5.7), have a mandate to explore ways to support better treatment of small and medium-sized enterprises (SME) research organisations and freelancers (Harkness and Hay 2025). There is an urgent need to update and properly advocate for equitable client commissioning of PAR projects, for example, through a revised code of conduct for commissioners (Social Research Association 2002; Hay and Harkness 2025).

> **Box 5.7: Meet the Mighty Mini Research Collective**
>
> The Mighty Mini Research Collective was set up in the autumn of 2024 by independent researchers Rowena Hay and Fran Harkness. It is a free-to-join, member-led network that now brings together 96 members through an active LinkedIn group and quarterly online lunch meetings. The collective is made up of independent researchers, freelancers, and micro-businesses, both new and established, who are not affiliated with a university, institution, or large organisation.
>
> The group focuses less on the research itself and more on the realities of *running* a small independent practice. Members support each other with business development, procurement practices, marketing, and navigating the lack of understanding about the real costs of independent research on both sides of the commissioning relationship. Common struggles include 'juggling all the hats' required to run a business and competing with larger players.
>
> The collective is run voluntarily and offers training, resources, best practice exchange, and networking opportunities. It also provides space for solidarity, wellbeing, and resilience – whether through sharing how it *feels* to work independently, running action learning sets, or developing shared advocacy. Plans are already underway to host a bottom-up conference in 2026, along with a prize to showcase members' work and strengthen their collective voice.
>
> To join the group, head to the following LinkedIn page: https://www.linkedin.com/groups/13115740/

Conclusion

In conclusion, we have outlined several ethical considerations that arise when conducting PAR. We, like others, believe that ethics cannot be a single 'tick-box' event, but rather an ongoing practice that we engage in throughout the entire research process. Moreover, ethics is not something we simply 'teach' community researchers, but something we collectively define and navigate together. We view ethics as fundamentally tied to power dynamics, which is why we have framed this chapter to emphasise the intentional stance that PAR projects take in attempting to reveal and destabilise existing power relationships. The pitfalls we have shared all illustrate the difficulties faced in navigating power in community researcher projects. We hope by sharing when things have gone wrong that others can reap the benefits and learn from our mistakes. We hope that this list of failures (and solutions) proves to be helpful for you in your own PAR endeavours.

6

Conclusion

This book has attempted to distil over 30 years of learning from practising PAR outside the university context, embedded in communities. We write at a time when PAR is enjoying renewed prominence in the UK. We are buoyed by this, but we have also 'been around the block' and know that past gains can be fragile. Institutional support ebbs and flows, and when it does, skills and knowledge are easily lost. In Chapter 5, we reflected on the precarity faced by independent researchers and PAR practitioners, like us, and the challenges of sharing and sustaining the work we do so that the practice is not lost and the learning can be widely shared.

This book traces the development of PAR in the UK beyond the university, highlighting its connections to community development. Our own experiences in Hull – a city on the margins – shape the perspective we bring to this work. We are fascinated by the parallels between global PAR roots, in pro-democratic movements in South America, international development contexts, in feminist and decolonial research practice, and the ways in which these resonate in left-behind UK communities. The work of local community-focused leaders like Gina Holdsworth, to whom this book is dedicated, demonstrates how passion, commitment, and local knowledge can transform practice.

Our exploration of literature on Eurocentric and colonial research reminds us that research has historically and continues to do damage in colonised communities. Many Indigenous communities, for example, see research as a 'dirty word'

(Tuhiwai Smith 1999), and communities in Hull often share similar frustrations: outsiders arrive, conduct research to advance their careers, are handsomely paid, and then depart, leaving communities with little benefit. Responsibility is too often shifted onto communities themselves, as if poverty or social inequality were the result of individual failings. This underscores the importance of PAR: vulnerability and marginality are not inherent traits, but are produced through policies and systems (Aldridge 2016). As Jo Aldridge (2016) rightly argues, research design should be carefully sculpted not to exacerbate vulnerability, but affirm participants' competence and agency.

Engaging with Indigenous ethics has been particularly enriching (Kara 2018). These approaches align far more closely with PAR than traditional top-down ethics committees, emphasising relationships, accountability, reciprocity, and benefit sharing (Weber-Pillwax 2001; Chilisa 2012). They have helped us reflect on our own practice and think more deeply about ethical design, power, and responsibility.

At the same time, this book provides a practical toolkit – a guide for people embarking on PAR to actually do it. It is structured around a clear PAR process, from planning and recruitment, through training, fieldwork, analysis, and action, to evaluation and closing projects well (Centre for Social Justice and Community Action 2012). None of this is rocket science, but it does require thought, reflection, and experimentation. Our hope is that readers will dip in and out of the book, taking what is useful for their own context, and – like our community researchers – have fun with the tools, adapt them creatively, be prepared to get it wrong, and see what works for their own people and places.

We have deliberately shared both successes and failures. PAR is not always easy; it is challenging for everyone involved. But these challenges are also opportunities: to develop skills, flex muscles of collaboration, and create spaces where community researchers can embed their knowledge and influence institutions. PAR enables tangible change, from improving services to better meet community needs, to empowering participants to act, to influencing local strategies and policy. Even small transformations such as new confidence, strengthened relationships, or creative outputs are valuable.

What makes PAR exciting and enduring is its flexibility. It is not a fixed set of tools or methods, but borrows from multiple traditions and adapts to context. We love seeing community researchers take ownership of PAR tools, shape them for their communities, and innovate in how findings are shared and acted upon. We are equally grateful for the creative collaborations that PAR allows, from song, drama, and illustration to interdisciplinary approaches, that enrich the process, broaden participation and reach.

Ultimately, this book is about learning, reflection, and sustaining practice. PAR works when it is ethical, iterative, flexible, and rooted in genuine collaboration. It thrives on relationships, respect, and shared responsibility. We hope that by sharing our history, insights, and practical tools, this book supports new and experienced PAR practitioners to continue the work, strengthen community voices, and keep the spirit and practice of PAR alive.

Notes

Chapter 1
1. Each of these categories does not exist in isolation; there is overlap between them. Communities tend to view their lives as a whole, not as a series of topics, activities, or service areas.

Chapter 2
1. Interestingly, recent scholarship has shown how PAR can be used as a way to critically analyse the use of artificial intelligence (AI) technologies both from a data (in)justice perspective (Medrado and Verdegem 2024) and as a way to evaluate its adoption as a tool to support efficiency in the delivery of public sector services (Sabater et al 2025).
2. Feminist scholarship is inherently action-oriented, seeking to understand patriarchal structures and promote positive social change and equality (Maguire 2006) As a political movement aimed at transforming social, structural, and personal aspects of society, it encourages researchers to consider gendered experiences and intersecting factors such as class and race (Gatenby and Humphries 2000; Harding and Norberg 2005; Maguire 2006, p 63).
3. https://jprm.scholasticahq.com/

Chapter 3
1. An example of one of these guides, this time for a project focused on women's access to information and support around gynaecological health, can be found linked here: https://www.canva.com/design/DAGliSJIugI/tJKHrmu4-HiH_rg7PyK9lA/view?utm_content=DAGliSJIugI&utm_campaign=designshare&utmmedium=link2&utmsource=uniquelinks&utlId=hb3525ca766

References

Adelman, C. 1993. 'Kurt Lewin and the origins of action research'. *Educational Action Research* 1(1): 7–24. doi: 10.1080/0965079930010102

Adeouye, A., Y. Clarke, R. Hay, R. Lamport, N. Lavithis, J. Molina, N. Mackie, et al. 2023. 'The past for the present: Community action research at Dulwich Picture Gallery'. https://www.dulwichpicturegallery.org.uk/media/12829/dpg_findings-report_final.pdf

Adriansen, H.K. 2012. 'Timeline interviews: A tool for conducting life history research'. *Qualitative Studies* 3(1): 40–55.

Al Hamwi, A., C. Keleşoğlu, K. Teklemariam, L. Agbaso, R. Puri, R. Newton, R. Hay et al. 2021. 'Refugee women's peer researcher project: Accessing information, rights and services in the UK'. https://www.shortwork.org.uk/projects/refugee-women's-peer-researcher-project%3A-accessing-rights-and-services-in-the-uk

Alasuutari, P., L. Bickman, and J. Brannen. eds. 2008. *The SAGE Handbook of Social Research Methods*. SAGE Publications.

Albary, E.M. and D.V. Eisma. 2021. 'Performance task assessment supported by the design thinking process: Results from a true experimental research'. *Social Sciences & Humanities Open* 3(1). doi: 10.1016/j.ssaho.2021.100116

Aldridge, J. 2016. *Participatory Research: Working with Vulnerable Groups in Research and Practice*. Policy Press.

Alevizou, G., K. Alexiou, and T. Zamenopoulos. 2016. 'Community asset mapping and related approaches for cultivating capacities'. Open University and AHRC. https://oro.open.ac.uk/47472/

Amin, A. 2005. 'Local community on trial'. *Economy and Society* 34(4): 612–633. doi: 10.1080/03085140500277211

Amsden, J., and R. VanWynsberghe. 2005. 'Community mapping as a research tool with youth'. *Action Research* 3(4): 357–381. doi: 10.1177/1476750305058487

Andersen, B., and T. Fagerhaug. 2006. *Root Cause Analysis: Simplified Tools and Techniques*. ASQ Quality Press.

Armstrong, A., K. Carter, H. Graham, P. Hayward, A. Henry, P. Holland, C. Holmes et al. 2013. 'Everyday ethics in community-based participatory research'. *Contemporary Social Science* 8(3): 263–277. doi: 10.1080/21582041.2013.769618

Arnstein, S.R. 1969. 'A ladder of citizen participation'. *Journal of the American Institute of Planners* 35(4): 216–244. doi: 10.1080/01944366908977225

Askins, K. 2008. 'In and beyond the classroom: Research ethics and participatory pedagogies'. *Area* 40(4): 500–509. https://www.jstor.org/stable/40346155

Baaz, M.E. 2005. *The Paternalism of Partnership: A Postcolonial Reading of Identity in Development Aid*. Zed Books.

Bagnoli, A. 2009. 'Beyond the standard interview: The use of graphic elicitation and arts-based methods'. *Qualitative Research* 9(5): 547–570.

Baker, E.A., F. Motton, E. Barnidge, and F. Rose III. 2013. 'Collaborative data collection, interpretation, and action planning in a rural African American community: Men on the move'. In *Methods for Community-Based Participatory Research for Health*, edited by B.A. Israel, E. Eng, A.J. Schulz, and E.A. Parker, E. A. (2nd ed.). Jossey-Bass, pp 435–462.

Banks, S., and M. Brydon-Miller. eds. 2018. *Ethics in Participatory Research for Health and Social Well-Being: Cases and Commentaries*. Taylor & Francis.

Banks, S., Armstrong, A., Carter, K., Graham, H., Hayward, P., Henry, A et al. 2013. 'Everyday ethics in community-based participatory research'. *Contemporary Social Science*, 8(3), 263–277. doi: 10.1080/21582041.2013.769618

Bell, E. 2006. 'Infusing Race into the US Discourse on Action Research'. In *Handbook of Action Research: Concise Paperback Edition*, edited by H. Bradbury. SAGE Publications, pp 49–59.

Bennett, F., and M. Roberts. 2004. *From Input to Influence: Participatory Approaches to Research and Inquiry into Poverty*. JRF.

Bennett, H. 2022. *Participatory Governance: Creating Space for Participatory Research or Crowding It Out?* Policy Alliance.

Berends, L. 2011. 'Embracing the visual: Using timelines with in-depth interviews on substance use and treatment'. *Qualitative Report* 16(1): 1–9.

Bertrand, M., S.M. Salinas, and D. Demps. 2020. '"It's everybody's job": Youth and adult constructions of responsibility to take action for school change through PAR'. *Urban Review* 52: 392–414. doi: 10.1007/s11256-019-00537-y

Beyer, H., and K. Holtzblatt. 1998. *Contextual Design: Defining Customer-Centered Systems.* Elsevier Science.

Billies, M., V. Francisco, P. Krueger, and D. Linville. 2010. 'Participatory Action Research: Our methodological roots'. *International Review of Qualitative Research* 3(3): 277–286. doi: 10.1525/irqr.2010.3.3.277

Boal, A. 2002. *Games for Actors and Non-actors.* Routledge.

Bradbury-Huang, H. 2010. 'What is good action research? Why the resurgent interest?' *Action Research* 8(1): 93–109. doi: 10.1177/1476750310362435

The Brain Charity. n.d. 'Physiotherapy through dance for people with dementia: Support for neurological conditions'. https://www.thebraincharity.org.uk/service/dementia/music-makes-us-move/

Braun, V., and V. Clarke. 2022. *Thematic Analysis: A Practical Guide.* SAGE Publications.

Brett-MacLean, P. 2009. 'Body mapping: Embodying the self living with HIV/AIDS'. *Canadian Medical Association Journal* 180(7): 740–741. http://www.cmaj.ca/content/180/7/740.full.pdf+html

British Museum. 2020. 'Positive action recruitment roadmap'. https://www.britishmuseum.org/sites/default/files/2020-03/Roadmap%20Report%20v5-link.pdf

Brown, G., S. Sanders, and P. Reed. 2018. 'Using public participatory mapping to inform general land use planning and zoning'. *Landscape and Urban Planning* 177: 64–74. doi: 10.1016/j.landurbplan.2018.04.011

Brown, N. 2024. *Photovoice Reimagined.* Policy Press.

Bryan, J. 2011. 'Walking the line: Participatory mapping, indigenous rights, and neoliberalism'. *Geoforum* 42(1): 40–50.

References

Burns, D., J. Howard, and S. Ospina. eds. 2021. *The SAGE Handbook of Participatory Research and Inquiry*. SAGE Publications.

Busza, J., and B.T. Schunter. 2001. 'From competition to community: Participatory learning and action among young, debt-bonded Vietnamese sex workers in Cambodia'. *Reproductive Health Matters* 9(17). doi: 10.1016/S0968-8080(01)90010-2

Cahill, C. 2007. 'The personal is political: Developing new subjectivities through participatory action research'. *Gender, Place & Culture*, 14(3), 267–292. doi: 10.1080/09663690701324904

Carrington, A., A. Denny, S. Dewfield, R. Fullegar, T. Gooda, R. Hay, R. Newton et al. 2025. *The Petworth Detectives: Community Action Research at Petworth House*. National Trust.

Cavestro, L. 2003. *P.R.A. – Participatory Rural Appraisal Concepts Methodologies and Techniques*. Universita 'Degli Studi di Padova Facolta' di Agraria.

Centre for Social Justice and Community Action. 2012. 'Community-based participatory research: A guide to ethical principles and practice'. https://www.publicengagement.ac.uk/resources/guide/community-based-participatory-research-guide-ethical-principles-and-practice

Centre for Social Justice and Community Action. 2022a. *Navigating Participatory Research: A Visual Guide*. UKRI.

Centre for Social Justice and Community Action. 2022b. Community-based participatory research A guide to ethical principles and practice (2nd edition). https://www.durham.ac.uk/media/durham-university/departments-/sociology/Community-Based-Participatory-Research-A-Guide-to-Ethical-Principles,-2nd-edition-(2022)-.pdf

Centre for Social Justice and Community Action. 2025. 'From the margins to the mainstream? Celebrating and challenging Participatory Action Research'. https://durham.ac.uk/research/institutes-and-centres/social-justice-community-action/about/events/participatory-action-research-conference-durham-11th-june-2025---/

Centre for Social Justice and Community Action. n.d. 'Participatory research innovation and learning - Innovation Lab I'. https://www.durham.ac.uk/research/institutes-and-centres/social-justice-community-action/about/events/participatory-research-innovation-and-learning---innovation-lab-i/

Chambers, R. 1981. 'Rapid rural appraisal: rationale and repertoire'. *Public Administration and Development* 1(2): 95–105.

Chambers, R. 1983. *Rural development: putting the last first.* Routledge.

Chambers, R. 1992. 'Rural appriasal: rapid, relaxed and participatory'. IDS Discussion Paper, no. 311.

Chambers, R. 1997. *Whose Reality Counts? Putting the First Last.* Intermediate Technology.

Chambers, R. 2002. *Participatory Workshops: A Sourcebook of 21 Sets of Ideas and Activities.* Earthscan.

Chambers, R. 2006. 'Participatory mapping and geographic information systems: Whose map? Who is empowered and who disempowered? Who gains and who loses?' *Electronic Journal of Information Systems in Developing Countries* 25: 1–11. doi: 10.1002/j.1681-4835.2006.tb00163.x.

Chambers, R. 2013. 'From rapid to reflective: 25 years of participatory learning and action'. In *Tools for Supporting Sustainable Natural Resource Management and Livelihoods*, edited by H, Ashley, N. Kenton, A. Milligan, pp 12–14, https://www.iied.org/14620iied

Chen, T. 2024. 'People-centred and participatory policymaking'. https://openpolicy.blog.gov.uk/2024/11/19/people-centred-and-participatory-policymaking/

Chilisa, B. 2012. *Indigenous Research Methodologies.* SAGE Publications.

Clarke, S., Blackman, R. and Carter, I. 2004. *Facilitation Skills Workbook.* Tearfund.

Cochrane, L., and J. Corbett. 2020. 'Participatory mapping'. In *Handbook of Communication for Development and Social Change.* Springer Singapore, pp 705–713.

Collins, A., and J. Wrigley. 2014. 'Can a neighbourhood approach to loneliness contribute to people's well-being?' JRF. https://www.housinglin.org.uk/_assets/Resources/Housing/OtherOrganisation/neighbourhood-loneliness-full.pdf

Contreras, S. 2019. 'Using Arnstein's ladder as an evaluative framework for the assessment of participatory work in postdisaster Haiti'. *Journal of the American Planning Association* 85(3): 213–235. doi: 10.1080/01944363.2019.1618728

Cook, S., and J. Corbett. 2019. 'Understanding gendered geographies of street homelessness using participatory mapping'. *Geomatica* 73(1): 81–92. doi: 10.1139/geomat-2019-0012

Cooke, B. 2004. 'Rules of thumb for participatory change agents'. In *Participation: From Tyranny to Transformation: Exploring New Approaches to Participation in Development,* edited by S. Hickey and G. Mohan. Bloomsbury Academic, pp 42–58.

Cooke, B., and U. Kothari. eds. 2001. *Participation: The New Tyranny?* Bloomsbury Academic

Corburn, J., A Y. Lee, N. Imara, and S. Swanston. 2013. 'Collaborative mapping for health equity'. In *Methods for Community-Based Participatory Research for Health*, edited by A.B. Israel, E. Eng, A.J. Schulz and E.A. Parker. Wiley, pp 463–488.

Cornwall, A., and R. Jewkes. 1995. 'What is participatory research?' *Social Science & Medicine* 41(12): 1667–1676.

Cornwall, A., and I. Scoones. eds. 2011. *Revolutionizing Development: Reflections on the Work of Robert Chambers*. Earthscan.

Crawford, K. 2024. 'Design thinking toolkit, activity 9 – Rose, Bud, Thorn'. https://spin.atomicobject.com/design-thinking-rose-bud-thorn/

Creative Facilitation. 2020. 'Line up (continuum)'. https://creativefacilitation.com/line-up-continuum-2/

Cruz, A.L. 2013. 'Paulo Freire's concept of concientizacao'. In *Paulo Freire's Intellectual Roots: Toward Historicity in Praxis*, edited by T. Kress and R. Lake. Bloomsbury Academic, pp 169–182.

Dancis, J.S., B.R. Coleman, and E.R. Ellison. 2023. 'Participatory Action Research as pedagogy: Stay messy'. *Journal of Participatory Research Methods* 4(2). doi: 10.35844/ 001c.75174

Davison, R.M., H. Chughtai, P. Nielsen, M. Marabelli, F. Iannacci, M. van Offenbeek et al. 2024. 'The ethics of using generative AI for qualitative data analysis'. *Information Systems Journal* 34(5): 1433–1439. doi: 10.1111/isj.12504

De Jager, A., A. Tewson, B. Ludlow, and K. Boydell. 2016. 'Embodied ways of storying the self: A systematic review of body-mapping'. *Forum: Qualitative Social Research* 17(2). https://openresearch.ocadu.ca/id/eprint/1206/

De Silva, G.V., P. Wignaraja, and M.A. Rahman. 1979. 'Bhoomi Sena: A struggle for people's power'. *Development Dialogue* 2: 3–70.

Deeb-Sossa, N. ed. 2019. *Community-Based Participatory Research: Testimonios from Chicana/o Studies*. University of Arizona Press.

Deng Deng, A., A. Gerrard, A. Casson, A. Ozedemir Kenar, A. Khalil, A. Hamde, E. Ahmed et al. 2019. 'Better births'. UCL. https://www.shortwork.org.uk/reports-and-downloads

Design Council. n.d.a. 'Framework for innovation'. https://www.designcouncil.org.uk/our-resources/framework-for-innovation/

Dixon, J., J. Ward, and S. Blower. 2019. '"They sat and actually listened to what we think about the care system": The use of participation, consultation, peer research and co-production to raise the voices of young people in and leaving care in England'. *Child Care in Practice* 25(1): 6–21. doi: 10.1080/13575279.2018.1521380

Dolaty, S., E. Midouhas, J. Deighton, and M.P. Somerville. 2025. 'Public participation in mental health programming: Insights into the ways young people are involved in the development, delivery, and evaluation of mental health initiatives in school and community spaces'. *International Journal of Adolescence and Youth* 30(1). doi: 10.1080/02673843.2025.2498616

Durham Community Research Team. 2022. 'Navigating participatory research: a visual guide'. Centre for Social Justice and Community Action, Durham University, UK.

Duxbury, N., W.F. Garrett-Petts, and D. MacLennan. eds. 2020. *Cultural Mapping as Cultural Inquiry*. Taylor & Francis.

Ehsassi, M.H. 2025. *Activated Citizenship: The Transformative Power of Citizens' Assemblies*. Routledge.

Eng, E., K. Strazza, S.D. Rhodes, D. Griffith, K. Shirah, and E. Mebane. 2013. 'Insiders and outsiders assess who is "the community"'. In *Methods for Community-Based Participatory Research for Health*, edited by A.B. Israel, E. Eng, A.J. Schulz and E.A. Parker. Wiley, pp 133–159.

England, K.V. 1994. 'Getting personal: Reflexivity, positionality, and feminist research'. *The Professional Geographer* 46(1): 80–89. doi: 10.1111/j.0033-0124.1994.00080.x

Escobar, A. 2011. *Encountering Development: The Making and Unmaking of the Third World*. Princeton University Press.

ESRC (Economic and Social Research Council). 2022. 'Framework for research ethics'. https://www.ukri.org/councils/esrc/guidance-for-applicants/research-ethics-guidance/framework-for-research-ethics/

Evaluation Support Scotland. 2019. 'ESS evaluation method: Evaluation wheel'. https://evaluationsupportscotland.org.uk/resources/evaluation-wheel/?utm_source=chatgpt.com

Evans, G. 2009. 'Accessibility, urban design and the whole journey environment'. *Built Environment* 35(3): 366–385. doi: 10.2148/benv.35.3.366

Fals Borda, O. 2006. 'Participatory (action) research in social theory: Origins and challenges'. In *The SAGE Handbook of Action Research: Participative Inquiry and Practice*, edited by P. Reason and H. Bradbury. SAGE Publications, pp 27–37.

Fals-Borda, O., and M.A. Rahman. eds. 1991. *Action and Knowledge: Breaking the Monopoly with Participatory Action Research*. Apex Press.

Fine, M. 2018. *Just Research in Contentious Times: Widening the Methodological Imagination*. Teachers College Press.

Fine, M., and M.E. Torre. 2021. *Essentials of Critical Participatory Action Research*. American Psychological Association.

Fitzgibbon, W. 2022. *Applied Photovoice in Criminal Justice: Voices Made Visible*. Taylor & Francis.

Freire, P. 2017. *Pedagogy of the Oppressed*, translated by M.B. Ramos. Penguin.

Folan, C. 2024. 'Embedding a user-centred design team into a policy area'. https://publicpolicydesign.blog.gov.uk/2024/01/04/embedding-a-user-centred-design-team-into-a-policy-area/

Gaber, J. 2019. 'Building "a ladder of citizen participation": Sherry Arnstein, citizen participation, and model cities'. *Journal of the American Planning Association* 85(3): 188–201. doi: 10.1080/01944363.2019.1612267

Gadotti, M., and C.A. Torres. 2009. 'Paulo Freire: Education for development'. *Development and Change* 40: 1255–1267. doi: 10.1111/j.1467-7660.2009.01606.x

Gaiser, L.E., and Y. Matras. 2021. 'Using smartphones to document linguistic landscapes: The LinguaSnapp mobile app'. *Linguistics Vanguard* 7(s1). doi: 10.1515/lingvan-2019-0012

Gastaldo, D., L. Magalhães, C. Carrasco, and C. Davy. 2012. 'Body-map storytelling as research: Methodological considerations for telling the stories of undocumented workers through body mapping'. http://www.migrationhealth.ca/undocumented-workers-ontario/body-mapping

Gatenby, B. and Humphries, M. 2000. 'Feminist participatory action research: Methodological and ethical issues'. *Women's Studies International Forum* 23(1): 89–105. doi: 10.1016/S0277-5395(99)00095-3

Gaventa, J., and A. Cornwall. 2008. 'Power and knowledge'. edited by P. Reason and H. Bradbury. SAGE Publications, pp 172–189, doi: 10.4135/9781848607934.n17

Genat, B. 2009. 'Building emergent situated knowledges in participatory action research'. *Action Research* 7(1): 101–115. doi: 10.1177/1476750308099600

Gibson, A.F., and A. Beattie. 2025. 'More or less than human? Evaluating the role of AI-as-participant in online qualitative research'. *Qualitative Research in Psychology* 21(2): 175–199. doi: 10.1080/14780887.2024.2311427

Greenbaum, S.D., G. Jacobs, and P. Zinn. eds. 2020. *Collaborating for Change: A Participatory Action Research Casebook*. Rutgers University Press.

Guhathakurta, M. 2015. 'Theatre in Participatory Action Research: Experiences from Bangladesh'. In *The SAGE Handbook of Action Research*, edited by H. Bradbury. SAGE Publications, pp 100–108.

Guijt, I., and M.K. Shah. eds. 1998. *The Myth of Community: Gender Issues in Participatory Development*. Intermediate Technology Publications.

Guta, A., S. Flicker, and B. Roche. 2010. *Peer Research in Action II: Management, Support, and Supervision*. Wellesley Institute.

Guy, S., and A.S. Inglis. 1999. 'Tips for trainers: Introducing the "H-Form" – a method for monitoring and evaluation'. *Learning from Analysis, Participatory Learning and Action Notes* 34: 84–87.

Harding, S., and Norberg, K. 2005. 'New Feminist Approaches to Social Science Methodologies: An Introduction'. *Signs* 30(4): 2009–2015. doi: 10.1086/428420

References

Harkness, F., and Hay, R. 2024. 'Mighty Mini Research Collective Kick Off_workshop summary'. https://docs.google.com/document/d/1ohzmAnW1srCwCg-MLvTXzoXQ1Q8rYxMpqqEDAdfInb8/edit?usp=sharing

Haraway, D. 1988. 'Situated knowledges: The science question in feminism and the privilege of partial perspective'. *Feminist Studies* 14(3): 575–599. doi: 10.2307/3178066

Hartlepool Action Lab. 2017. *Making Life Affordable: A Community Research Report about the Cost of Living in Hartlepool.* Hartlepool Action Lab and JRF.

Harju, A., I.M. Bernedo Muñoz, and D. Tofteng. 2024. 'Tensions and dilemmas in participatory youth projects working within institutional frameworks'. *International Journal of Adolescence and Youth* 29(1). doi: 10.1080/02673843.2024.2312855

Harris, E. 2025. *Encountering the World with I-Docs: Interactive Documentary as a Research Method.* Bristol University Press

Hart, R. 1992. 'Children's participation: From tokenism to citizenship'. *Innocenti Essay* 92(6).

Hartlepool Mail. 2016. 'New communtiy programme aims to tackle poverty issues'. https://www.hartlepoolmail.co.uk/news/new-community-programme-aims-to-help-tackle-hartlepool-poverty-issues-395523

Haste, A., and L. Baines. eds. 2024. *Guide for Independent Scholars.* National Coalition of Independent Scholars.

Hay, R. 2018. The *Community Insights Programme.* Shortwork.

Hay, R., and F. Harkness. 2025. 'Independent futures: why micro social researchers need a collective voice'. *Research Matters* (March). https://the-sra.org.uk/SRA/SRA/Publications/Research-Matters.aspx

Hay, S. 2008. *SOS Gangs Project, Camberwell.* Cadbury Trust and University of Kent.

Hay, S. 2013. *Don't Want to Talk about It: Accessing Cancer Screening in Tower Hamlets.* Women's Health and Family Services and Tower Hamlets Public Health.

Hay, S. 2014a. Community based perspectives and solutions relating to Type 2 Diabetes and associated lifestyles on the Aberfeldy Estate. London Borough of Tower Hamlets.

Hay, S. 2014b. Health and Wellbeing in the Workplace. Poplar HARCA and Shortwork.

Hay, S. 2014c. Social Asset Mapping for Health. London Borough of Tower Hamlets.

Hay, S. 2014d. South Hampstead Community Action Centre - Quality of Life Project. Shortwork.

Hay, S. 2015. Experiences of people with Dual Diagnosis in Tower Hamlets: A participatory research project conducted by Providence Row Housing Association's Peer Consultancy Team. Providence Row Housing Association.

Healthcare Improvement Scotland. n.d. 'Head, heart, bag and bin'. https://www.hisengage.scot/engaging-communities/participation-toolkit/head-heart-bag-and-bin/

Herr, K., and G.L. Anderson. 2005. 'The continuum of positionality in action research'. In *The Action Research Dissertation: A Guide for Students and Faculty*. SAGE Publications, pp 29–48.

Hickey, S. and Mohan, G. (eds) 2004. *Participation: From Tyranny to Transformation?: Exploring New Approaches to Participation in Development*. Zed Books.

Howard, J., and M. Tadros. eds. 2023. *Using Participatory Methods to Explore Freedom of Religion and Belief: Whose Reality Counts?* Bristol University Press.

Huff, D. 1991. *How to Lie with Statistics*. Penguin.

Hunsberger, C., and W. Kenyon. 2008. 'Action planning to improve issues of effectiveness, representation and scale in public participation: A conference report'. *Journal of Public Deliberation* 4(1): 1–18.

Hurtubise, K., and R. Joslin. 2023. 'Participant-generated timelines: A participatory tool to explore young people with chronic pain and parents' narratives of their healthcare experiences'. *Qualitative Health Research* 33(11): 931–944. doi: 10.1177/10497323231189388.

Huss, E., R. Kaufman, A. Avgar, and E. Shouker. 2015. 'Using arts-based research to help visualize community intervention in international aid'. *International Social Work* 58(5): 673–688.

ICA-International. n.d. 'ToP faciliation'. https://www.ica-international.org/top-facilitation/

ICA:UK. 2014. 'Consensus workshop method overview'. https://www.google.com/url?sa=t&source=web&rct=j&opi=89978449&url=https://ica-uk.org.uk/wp-content/uploads/2020/04/Consensus-Workshop-Overview.pdf&ved=2ahUKEwjyh5-x28uQAxUNWkEAHeuQFCMQFnoECBgQAQ&usg=AOvVaw2HNKwCdfCO7l5sM2wcUBDZ

ICPHR (International Collaboration for Participatory Health Research). 2022. *Position Paper 2: Participatory Health Research – A Guide to Ethical Principles and Practice*. ICPHR.

Ishikawa, K. 1982. *Guide to Quality Control*. Asian Productivity Organization.

Imrie, R., and M. Raco. eds. 2003. *Urban Renaissance? New Labour, Community and Urban Policy*. Policy Press.

Involve. n.d. 'Citizens' jury'. https://www.involve.org.uk/resource/citizens-jury

Ishkanian, A., and S. Szreter. eds. 2012. *The Big Society Debate: A New Agenda for Social Welfare?* Edward Elgar.

Israel, B.A., E. Eng, A.J. Schulz, and E.A. Parker. eds. 2013. *Methods for Community-Based Participatory Research for Health*. Wiley.

Jhun, N.K., Z. Shari, and M. Hassan. 2025. 'Exploring stakeholders' perceptions and priorities in promoting social sustainability through building design and public participation: A case study in Malaysia'. *International Journal of Urban Sustainable Development* 17(1): 1–19.

Jokela-Pansini, M., and B. Greenough. 2024. 'When you can't find the words: Using body mapping to communicate patients' experiences of long Covid'. *Health & Place* 89. doi: 10.1016/j.healthplace.2024.103302.

Jones, G., R. Meegan, P. Kennett, and J. Croft. 2015. The uneven impact of austerity on the voluntary and community sector: A tale of two cities. *Urban Studies* 53(10): 2064–2080. doi: 10.1177/0042098015587240

Jones, C. 1995. *Participatory Appraisal Workshop Proceedings*. Department of Public Health, University of Hull.

Jones, O. 2020. *Chavs: The Demonization of the Working Class*. Verso.

JRF (Joseph Rowntree Foundation). 2014. *Neighbourhood Approaches to Loneliness*. JRF.

JRF. 2025. 'New JRF modelling shows scale of living standards assault on poorest who are set to see incomes fall twice as fast by end of Parliament'. https://www.jrf.org.uk/news/new-jrf-modelling-shows-scale-of-living-standards-assault-on-poorest

Kapoor, I. 2008. *The Postcolonial Politics of Development*. Taylor & Francis.

Kara, H. 2018. *Research Ethics in the Real World: Euro-Western and Indigenous Perspectives*. Policy Press.

Kara, H., and L. Baines. 2023. 'If UKRI wants to support a diverse research environment, it should include independent researchers'. https://blogs.lse.ac.uk/impactofsocialsciences/2023/05/19/if-ukri-wants-to-support-a-diverse-research-environment-it-should-include-independent-researchers/

Kara, H., K.J. Gergen, and M. Gergen. 2020. *Creative Research Methods: A Practical Guide*. Policy Press.

Keith, M.M., and J.T. Brophy. 2004. 'Participatory mapping of occupational hazards and disease among asbestos-exposed workers from a foundry and insulation complex in Canada'. *International Journal of Occupational and Environmental Health* 10(2): 144–153.

Kesby, M. 2000. 'Participatory diagramming: Deploying qualitative methods through an action research epistemology'. *Area* 32(4): 423–435.

Kindon, S. 2005. 'Participatory action research'. In *Qualitative Research Methods in Human Geography*, edited by I. Hay. Oxford University Press, pp 207–220.

Kindon, S. Pain, R. and Kesby, M. 2007. *Participatory Action Research Approaches and methods: Connecting People, Participation and Place*. Routledge.

Kindon, S.L., M. Kesby, and R. Pain. eds. 2024. *Critically Engaging Participatory Action Research*. Routledge.

Kindon, S.L., R. Pain, and M. Kesby. eds. 2007. *Participatory Action Research Approaches and Methods: Connecting People, Participation and Place*. Routledge.

Kloppenborg, K., M. Price Ball, S. Jonas, G.I. Wolf, and B. Greshake Tzovaras. 2024. 'Co-designing a wiki-based community knowledge management system for personal science'. *Royal Society Open Science* 11(7). doi: 10.1098/rsos.240275

Kolar, K., F. Ahmad, L. Chan, and P.G. Erickson. 2015. 'Timeline mapping in qualitative interviews: A study of resilience with marginalized groups'. *International Journal of Qualitative Methods* 14(3): 13–32. doi: 10.1177/160940691501400302

Ledwith, M. 2016. *Community Development in Action: Putting Freire into Practice*. Policy Press.

Ledwith M., and J. Springett. 2022. *Participatory Practice: Community-Based Action for Transformative Change*. Policy Press.

Lewin, K. 1948. *Resolving Social Conflict: Selected Papers on Group Dynamics*. Facsimile Publisher.

Lichten, C., R. Ioppolo, C. D'Angelo, R.K. Simmons, and M. Jones. 2018. *Citizen Science: Crowdsourcing for Research*. THIS Institute.

Lichtenstein, R., D. Hay, P. Guillery, and L. Vaughan. 2020. 'A memory map of the Jewish East End'. Bartlett Faculty of the Built Environment, UCL. https://jewisheastendmemorymap.org/

Local Trust. 2015. 'Community-research-in-big-local-areas'. https://localtrust.org.uk/news-and-stories/blog/community-research-in-big-local-areas/

Local Trust. 2025. 'Big local'. https://localtrust.org.uk/big-local/

Ludlow, B. 2014. 'Witnessing: Creating visual research memos about patient experiences of body mapping in a dialysis unit'. *American Journal of Kidney Diseases* 64(5) xiii–xiv.

Lykes, M.B. 2006. 'Creative arts and photography in Participatory Action Research in Guatemala'. In *Handbook of Action Research: Concise Paperback Edition*, edited by P. Reason and H. Bradbury. SAGE Publications, pp 269–278.

Maguire, P. 2006. 'Uneven ground: Feminisms and action research'. In *Handbook of Action Research: Concise Paperback Edition*, edited by H. Bradbury. SAGE Publications, pp 269–278.

Manchester School of Architecture. 2025. 'Co-creating age-friendly social housing – Manchester School of Architecture'. https://www.msa.ac.uk/research/co-creating-age-friendly-social-housing/

Mannay, D. 2021. 'Visualizing pasts, futures and the present: How can creative research methods enable reflection, reflexivity and imagination? In *Temporality in Qualitative Inquiry: Theories, Methods and Practices*, edited by B.C. Clift, J. Gore, S. Gustafsson, S. Bekker, I.C Batlle and J. Hatchard Routledge, pp. 127–141.

Martin, B., and B. Hanington. 2012. *Universal Methods of Design: 100 Ways to Research Complex Problems, Develop Innovative Ideas, and Design Effective Solutions*. Rockport Publishers.

Marshall, T. n.d. 'Citizen science projects'. https://www.wildlifetrusts.org/citizen-science

Martikke, S., A. Church, and A. Hart. 2015. *Greater Than the Sum of Its Parts: What Works in Sustaining Community-University Partnerships*. GMCVO.

Mathers, S. 2010. 'Developing participatory research in radiology: The use of a graffiti wall, cameras and a video box in a Scottish radiology department'. *Pediatric Radiology* 40: 309–317.

Mayo, P. 2017. 'Praxis'. In *Encyclopaedia of Educational Philosophy and Theory*. Dordrecht: Springer, pp 1946–1951.

McNiff, J. 2013. *Action Research: Principles and Practice*. Routledge.

McTaggart, R. ed. 1997. *Participatory Action Research: International Contexts and Consequences*. State University of New York Press.

Medrado, A., and P. Verdegem. 2024. 'Participatory Action Research in critical data studies: Interrogating AI from a South–North approach'. *Big Data & Society* 11(1). doi: 10.1177/20539517241235869.

Mead, M. 1943. 'The factor of food habits'. *Annals of the American Academy of Political and Social Science* 225: 136–141. https://www.jstor.org/stable/1023547

Merton, R.K. 1972. 'Insiders and outsiders: A chapter in the sociology of knowledge'. *American Journal of Sociology* 78(1): 9–47. http://www.jstor.org/stable/2776569

Mienczakowski, J., and S. Morgan. 2001. 'Ethnodrama: Constructing participatory, experiential and compelling action research through performance'. In *Handbook of Action Research: Concise Paperback Edition*, edited by P. Reason and H. Bradbury. SAGE Publications, pp 219–227.

Michalko, M. 2006. *Thinkertoys: A Handbook of Creative-Thinking Techniques*. Clarkson Potter/Ten Speed.

Michigan Medicine. 2024. 'Michigan Body Map (MBM)'. https://medicine.umich.edu/dept/pain-research/clinical-research/michigan-body-map-mbm

Mighty Mini Research Collective. n.d. 'Mighty Mini Research Collective'. https://www.linkedin.com/groups/13115740/

Mitchell, C. 2011. *Doing Visual Research*. Sage.

Minkler M. 2005. 'Community-based research partnerships: Challenges and opportunities'. *J Urban Health* 82(2 Suppl 2): ii3–ii12. doi: 10.1093/jurban/jti034

Monk, J. 2007. 'Preface'. In *Participatory Action Research Approaches and Methods: Connecting People, Participation and Place*, edited by S.L. Kindon, R. Pain, and M. Kesby. Routledge, pp xxiii–xxiv.

Morgan, J. and Bambanani Women's Group. 2003. *Long Life: Positive HIV Stories*. Double Storey.

Munck, R., L. McIlrath, B. Hall, and R. Tandon. 2014. *Higher Education and Community-Based Research*. Palgrave Macmillan.

Murad M.H., Asi, N., Alsawas, M. et al. 2016. 'New evidence pyramid'. *Evidence-Based Medicine* 21: 125–127.

National Institute for Health and Care Research. 2014. 'Payment guidance for researchers and professionals involving people in research'. https://www.nihr.ac.uk/payment-guidance-researchers-and-professionals

National Lottery Community Fund. 2025. 'Participatory grantmaking (PGM)'. Available at: https://www.tnlcommunityfund.org.uk/insights/grantmaking-practice/grantmaking-practice/participatory-grantmaking-practice

Natow, R.S. 2022. 'Policy actors' perceptions of qualitative research in policymaking: The case of higher education rulemaking in the United States'. *Evidence & Policy* 18(1): 109–126. doi: 10.1332/174426420X16047229138089

Newman, K., 2008. 'Whose view matters? Using participatory processes to evaluate "Reflect" in Nigeria'. *Community Development Journal*, 43(3): 382–394. https://ssrn.com/abstract=1153896 or http://dx.doi.org/bsn015

Newman, G., D. Zimmerman, A. Crall, M. Laituri, J. Graham, and L. Stapel. 2010. 'User-friendly web mapping: Lessons from a citizen science website'. *International Journal of Geographical Information Science* 24(12): 1851–1869. doi: 10.1080/13658816.2010.490532

Newton, R., and R. Puri. 2023. Hackney Youth Project. 3Ps. http://3ps.org.uk/wp-content/uploads/2023/11/Hackney-Youth-project-final-report271123.pdf

NHS. n.d. 'Patient and public involvement'. https://www.england.nhs.uk/aac/what-we-do/patient-and-public-involvement/

NHS England. 2017. 'Patient and public participation in commissioning health and care: statutory guidance for CCGs and NHS England'. https://www.england.nhs.uk/publication/patient-and-public-participation-in-commissioning-health-and-care-statutory-guidance-for-ccgs-and-nhs-england/

O'Brien, C., and Divine, C. 2023. 'Body mapping refugees and asylum seekers' perspectives of embodied trauma: An innovative method for psychotraumatology research & practice'. *Qualitative Research in Psychology* 21(1): 71–106. doi: 10.1080/14780887.2023.2289964

O'Neill, G. 2015. *Curriculum Design in Higher Education: Theory to Practice*. UCD Teaching & Learning.

Oxfam. 2001. 'Oxfam UKPP's Partners' Participatory Appraisal Review Workshop'. https://oxfamilibrary.openrepository.com/bitstream/handle/10546/112328/oxfam-ukpp%27s-partners%27-participatory-appraisal-review-workshop-070604-en.pdf?sequence=1&isAllowed=y

Ozbil Torun, A., I. Akin, M. Defeyter, and Y. Severcan. 2024. 'Children's perspectives of neighbourhood spaces: Gender-based insights from participatory mapping and GIS analysis'. *Urban Planning* 9(8499). doi: 10.17645/up.8499

Pahl, K., R. Steadman-Jones, and L. Vasudevan. 2023. *Collaborative Research in Theory and Practice: The Poetics of Letting Go*. Bristol University Press.

Pain, R., G. Whitman, D. Milledge, and Lune Rivers Trust. 2011. *Participatory Action Research Toolkit*. Durham University.

Pala, A. 1978. *Women's Access to Land and Their Role in Agriculture and Decision-Making on the Farm: Experience of the Joluo of Kenya*. Nairobi, Kenya. Institute for Development Studies.

Parker, P. 2018. *The Art of Gathering: Create Transformative Meetings, Events and Experiences*. Riverhead Books.

Parme, S. 2014. 'Improving library orientation (and more) based on graffiti wall student surveys'. *LOEX Quarterly* 42(2): 2–10. https://commons.emich.edu/loexquarterly/vol42/iss2/2

Pasmore, W. 2006. 'Action research in the workplace: The socio-technical perspective'. In *Handbook of Action Research: Concise Paperback Edition*, edited by P. Reason and H. Bradbury. SAGE Publications, pp 38–48.

Patel, L. 2016. *Decolonizing Educational Research: From Ownership to Answerability*. Routledge.

Pink, S. 2012. *Advances in Visual Methodology*. Sage Publications.

Pola, R. 2024. 'Research in Kenya'. https://light.lstmed.ac.uk/research/research-in-kenya

Pretty, J.N. 1995. *A Trainer's Guide for Participatory Learning and Action*. Sustainable Agriculture Programme, International Institute for Environment and Development.

Quaker Social Action. 2018. 'Head, heart, bag, bin!' https://quakersocialaction.org.uk/sites/default/files/field/attachments/9.%20Head,%20Heart,%20Bag,%20Bin%20handout%206%20MTCN%20NEW.pdf /

Rainforest Foundation. 2020. 'Participatory mapping'. https://www.mappingforrights.org/participatory-mapping/

Rappaport, J. 2020. *Cowards Don't Make History: Orlando Fals Borda and the Origins of Participatory Action Research*. Duke University Press.

Reason, P., and H. Bradbury. eds. 2006. *Handbook of Action Research: Concise Paperback Edition*. SAGE Publications.

Rees, J., L. Caulfield, J. Booth, B. Sojka, K. Spicksley, J. Blamire, and E. Arnull. 2024. 'The opportunities, challenges, and rewards of "community peer research": Reflections on research practice'. *Qualitative Inquiry*. doi: 10.1177/10778004241229789

Rezvani, S., E. Duffy, R. Hay, and M. Ramagavigan. 2025. *Retrofit for All*. Carbon Coop.

Rocha, E.M. 1997. 'A ladder of empowerment'. *Journal of Planning Education and Research* 17(1). doi 10.1177/0739456X97017001.

Rose, G. 1997. 'Situating knowledges: Positionality, reflexivities and other tactics'. *Progress in Human Geography* 21(3): 305–320. doi: 10.1191/030913297673302122

Rossman, G.B., and S.F. Rallis. 2010. 'Everyday ethics: Reflections on practice'. *International Journal of Qualitative Studies in Education* 23(4): 379–391. doi: 10.1080/09518398.2010.492813

Rowe, W.E. 2014. 'Positionality'. In *The SAGE Encyclopedia of Action Research*, edited by D. Coghlan and M. Brydon-Miller. SAGE Publications, pp 628–628.

Rowley, J., M. Doyle, and S. Hay. 2013. 'Can we define ethical standards for participatory work?' In *Tools for Supporting Sustainable Natural Resource Management and Livelihoods*, edited by H. Ashley, N. Kenton, and A. Milligan. IIED, pp 91–100.

Ryan, F. 2019. *Crippled: Austerity and the Demonization of Disabled People*. Verso.

Rye, S.A., and N.I. Kurniawan. 2017. 'Claiming Indigenous rights through participatory mapping and the making of citizenship'. *Political Geography* 61: 148–159. doi: 10.1016/j.polgeo.2017.08.008

Sabater, A., B. López, R. Campdepadrós, and C. Sánchez. 2025. 'Participatory Action Research for AI in social services: An example of local practices from Catalonia'. In *Participatory Artificial Intelligence in Public Social Services: From Bias to Fairness in Assessing Beneficiaries*, edited by P. Ahrweiler. Springer Nature Switzerland, pp 79–96.

Sadanandan, S., P. Natarajan, J. Antony, and V.P. Vipinkumar. 2007. *Data Tools: Participatory Rural Appraisal Techniques*. Cohin University of Science and Technology.

Sathorar, H., and D. Geduld. 2021. 'A critical approach to university-community partnerships: Reflecting on the diverse realities'. *Educational Research for Social Change* 10(2): 88–104. doi: 10.17159/2221-4070/2021/v10i2a6

Saunders, T., H. Goulden, and D. Chapman. 2024. 'Why we need community research networks'. https://www.ukri.org/blog/why-we-need-community-research-networks/

School for Social Entrepreneurs. n.d. 'The School for Social Entrepreneurs'. https://www.the-sse.org/

Schultz, R.L. 2006. *Hull-House Maps and Papers: A Presentation of Nationalities and Wages in a Congested District of Chicago, Together with Comments and Essays on Problems Growing out of the Social Conditions*. University of Illinois Press.

Scottish Executive. 2009. 'Consultation toolkit: A practical guide to consulting with children and young people on policy related issues'. https://resourcecentre.savethechildren.net/document/consultation-toolkit-practical-guide-consulting-children-and-young-people-policy-related/

Sellers, T., and M. Westerby. 1996. 'Teenage facilitators: Barriers to improving adolescent sexual health'. *PLA Notes* 25: 77–80.

Seppälä, T., M. Sarantou, and S. Miettinen. eds. 2021. *Arts-Based Methods for Decolonising Participatory Research*. Routledge.

Shah, M.K., S.D. Kambou, and B. Monahan. 1999. *Embracing Participation in Development: Wisdom from the Field*. Care, Health and Population Unit.

Sheridan, J., K. Chamberlain, and A. Dupuis. 2011. 'Timelining: Visualizing experience'. *Qualitative Research* 11: 552–570.

Skelton, D. 2024. 'Hartlepool Action Lab: Local people working together to solve poverty'. https://atd-uk.org/2024/02/15/hartlepool-action-lab-local-people-working-together-to-solve-poverty/

Slotterback, C.S., and M. Lauria. 2019. 'Building a foundation for public engagement in planning: 50 years of impact, interpretation, and inspiration from Arnstein's ladder'. *Journal of the American Planning Association* 85(3): 183–187. doi: 10.1080/01944363.2019.1616985

Smith, L., C. Carr, I. Chesher, and L. Phillipson. 2023. 'The meaning of home when you don't live there anymore: Using body mapping with people with dementia in care homes'. *Ageing & Society* 1–26. doi: 10.1017/S0144686X23000259

Sport England. n.d. 'Participatory tools for community sport hubs and sport clubs. Tool 8: Evaluation wheel'. https://share.google/0VyvqM5CMVBfm8l5r

SRA (Social Research Association). 2002. *Commissioning Social Research: A Good Practice Guide*. https://share.google/Lbu1aq7PXZLagEMCo

SRA. 2001. 'Ethical guidelines'. https://the-sra.org.uk/SRA/SRA/Ethics/Research-Ethics-Guidance.aspx

Stack, E.E., and K. McDonald. 2018. 'We are "both in charge, the academics and self-advocates": Empowerment in community-based participatory research'. *Journal of Policy and Practice in Intellectual Disabilities*. doi: 10.1111/jppi.12236

Starr, M., S. Wallace, C. Moore, B. Cockrum, B. Hawryluk, A. Carroll, and W. Bennett. 2023. 'Development of a family-centered communication tool for kidney health in premature infants Qualitative focus group study using human-centered design methodology'. *Journal of Participatory Medicine* 15. doi: 10.2196/45316

Stein Greenberg, S. 2021. *Creative Acts for Curious People: How to Think, Create, and Lead in Unconventional Ways*. Clarkson Potter/Ten Speed.

Steps Centre. 2016. 'Methods vignettes: Evaluation H'. https://steps-centre.org/pathways-methods-vignettes/methods-vignettes-evaluation-h/

Stoecker, R., and A. Falcón. eds. 2022. *Handbook on Participatory Action Research and Community Development*. Edward Elgar.

Stokke, K. and Mohan, G. 2001. 'The convergence around local civil society and the dangers of localism'. *Social Scientist* 29(11/12): 3–24. doi:10.2307/3518224

Stuart, K., and L. Maynard. 2022. *The Practitioner Guide to Participatory Research with Groups and Communities*. Policy Press.

Sturge, G. 2022. *Bad Data: How Governments, Politicians and the Rest of Us Get Misled by Numbers*. Little, Brown.

Sullivan-Wiley, K.A., A.G. Short Gianotti, and J.P. Casellas Connors. 2019. 'Mapping vulnerability: Opportunities and limitations of participatory community mapping'. *Applied Geography* 105: 47–57. doi: 10.1016/j.apgeog.2019.02.008

Sutcliffe, P., R. Leaver, and M. Mouameletzi. 2025. 'Empathetic chatbots and synthetic personas – how AI is shaping research?' Presentation at the SRA Conference, Royal College of Physicians, London, 9 July.

Swantz, M.-L., E. Ndedya, and M.S. Masaiganah. 2006. 'Participatory Action Research in southern Tanzania, with special reference to women'. In *Handbook of Action Research*. SAGE Publications, pp 286–296.

Swords, J., M. Jeffries, H. East, and S. Messer. 2019. 'Mapping the city: Participatory mapping with young people'. *Geography* 104(3): 141–147. doi: 10.1080/00167487.2019.12094077

Thompson, S. (2025) *Skills Development of Early Career Researchers Involved in Disability-Inclusive Arts and Humanities Research*, Institute of Development Studies, doi: 10.19088/IDS.2025.020

Thompson, S., and M. Cannon. 2023. 'Power, poverty, and knowledge: Reflecting on 50 years of learning with Robert Chambers'. *IDS Bulletin* 54(1A). doi: 10.19088/1968-2023.112.

Toliver, S.R. 2021. *Recovering Black Storytelling in Qualitative Research: Endarkened Storywork*. Taylor & Francis.

References

Toubajie J., N. East, N. Lavithis, S. Dewfield, S. Mohideen, and T. Okeke. 2024. *Camden Streets Engagement*. Camden Council and Shortwork.

Tower Hamlets Council. n.d. 'Community Insights Network'. https://www.towerhamletstogether.com/our-work/community-insights-network.

Toynbee Hall. 2021. *Rent-Move-Repeat*. Toynbee Hall.

Toynbee Hall. 2023. 'Celebrating five years of using Participatory Action Research as a tool for social change'. https://www.toynbeehall.org.uk/12/01/2023/celebrating-5-years-of-using-participatory-action-research-as-a-tool-for-social-change/

Tuhiwai Smith, L. 1999. *Decolonizing Methodologies: Research and Indigenous Peoples*. Zed Books.

UK Participatory Research Network. n.d. 'UK Participatory Research Network'. https://ukprn.weebly.com/

UKRI (UK Research and Innovation). 2025. 'Co-production in research – UKRI'. https://www.ukri.org/manage-your-award/good-research-resource-hub/research-co-production/

UKRI. 2024a. 'Guidance on payment for public partners'. https://www.ukri.org/publications/payment-for-public-partners/guidance-on-payment-for-public-partners/

UKRI. 2024b. 'Investment to address regional priorities with UK communities'. https://www.ukri.org/news/investment-to-address-regional-priorities-with-uk-communities/

Unger, R., and C. Chandler. 2009. *A Project Guide to UX Design: For User Experience Designers in the Field or in the Making*. New Riders.

University of Liverpool. n.d. 'Participatory research funding'. https://www.liverpool.ac.uk/health-and-life-sciences/engage-with-us/public-engagement/opportunities-and-support/funding/participatory-research-funding/

University of Oxford. n.d. 'Participatory research: Strengthening research outcomes by involving the communities and users of research'. https://www.glam.ox.ac.uk/participatory-research

Valentine, G., and C. Harris. 2014. 'Strivers vs skivers: Class prejudice and the demonisation of dependency in everyday life'. *Geoforum* 53: 84–92. doi: 10.1016/j.geoforum.2014.02.007

Van der Heijden, M., and C. Collie. 2025. 'From informing to co-producing: A comparative analysis of citizen participation in missing persons cold cases in England & Wales and the Netherlands using the citizen participation ladder model'. *International Journal of Comparative and Applied Criminal Justice* 49(3): 195–213.

Vanderbilt University. n.d. 'Community research action PhD'. Vanderbilt University. https://peabody.vanderbilt.edu/academics/phd-programs/community-research-action-phd/

Vaughn, L.M., and F. Jacquiz. 2020. 'Participatory research methods: Choice points in the research process'. *Journal of Participatory Research Methods* 1(1). doi: 10.35844/ 001c.13244

Wadsworth, Y. 1998. 'What is Participatory Action Research?' *Action Research International* 2. http://www.scu.edu./schools/gem/ar/ari/p-ywadsworth98.html

Walker, P. 2020. 'Carousel technique: One for your toolbox'. https://www.penny-walker.co.uk/blog/2020/1/30/carousel-technique-one-for-your-toolbox

Wang, C., Burris, M.A. 1997. 'Photovoice: concept, methodology, and use for participatory needs assessment'. Health Educ Behav. 24(3): 369–387. doi: 10.1177/109019819702400309

Warwick-Booth, L., A.-M. Bagnall, and S. Coan. 2021. *Creating Participatory Research: Principles, Practice and Reality*. Policy Press.

Weber-Pillwax, C. (2001). 'What is Indigenous research?' *Canadian Journal of Native Education*, 25(2), 166–174.

West, E. 1999. *The Big Book of Icebreakers: Quick, Fun Activities for Energizing Meetings and Workshops*. McGraw-Hill Education.

Westerby, M., and S. Hay. 2010. *Safeguarding in Camden Communities*. Camden Safeguarding Board.

Worthen, M., A. Veale, and M. Wessells. 2019. 'The transformative and emancipatory potential of participatory evaluation: Reflections from a participatory action research study with war-affected young mothers'. *Oxford Development Studies* 47(2): 154–170. doi: 10.1080/13600818.2019.1584282

Yang, C., and Z. Dibb. 2020. *Peer Research in the UK*. Institute for Community Studies. https://www.youngfoundation.org/institute-for-community-studies/repository/peer-research-in-the-uk/#ICS-WP-Peer-Research-in-the-UK.pdf

Young Foundation. 2024a. 'Community Research Networks'. https://www.youngfoundation.org/community-research-networks/

Young Foundation. 2024b. 'Ten principles of peer research'. https://www.youngfoundation.org/peer-research-network/about/ten-principles-of-peer-research/

Young Foundation. n.d.a. 'Institute for Community Studies'. https://www.youngfoundation.org/institute-for-community-studies/

Young Foundation. n.d.b. 'What is peer research?' https://www.youngfoundation.org/research/what-is-peer-research/

Zuber-Skerritt, O. 1996. *Action Research for Change and Development*. Routledge.

Index

References to figures appear in *italic* type;
those in **bold** type refer to tables.

A

accessibility, and community researcher training 69
accountability 131, 140, 152
action (PAR process stage) 84
  enacting change 87–92
  reporting and feedback 84–87
  Timelines 112
action planning tools 100, 127
  Bean Counter 128–129, *129*
  Criteria Ranking 100, 129, *129*
  Impact Criteria 128
  Impact Matrix 128, 129–131, *130*
  ranking and scoring tools 127–131, *128*, *129*
Action Research 15
  action-reflection cycle 15, 42, 57
active listening 64
adaptability, in workshop design techniques 76
Adeouye, Adeolu 19, 79
advocacy 5, 68, 158
affinity clustering *125*, 125–127
Agbaso, Larysa 67
age, and mapping 105–106
Aldridge, J. 139, 161
All Party Parliamentary Group on Poverty 32
analysis 100, 123–124
  affinity clustering *125*, 125–127
  collaborative 82–84
  H-Forms 81, 82, 92, 100, 116–119, *117*
  Rose-Bud-Thorn tool 81–82, 92, *124*, 124–125, 126
'anti-saboteur' measures 31, 108, 150
  Anti-saboteur role 75

Arnstein, Sherry 11, 16–18, 41, 43
  and community researchers 18, 20–21
Art-Based Methods for Decolonising Participatory Research (Seppälä, Sarantou and Miettinen) 26
Art of Gathering, The (Parker) 69
arts, the 3, 26, 51
  PAR projects in 6
  Petworth House 85–87
  see also creative methods
asylum seekers 7
  see also refugees
austerity policies 9, 32–33, 36, 41

B

Baines, L. 157
Ball, Jonathan 123
Banks, S. 35, 138, 139
Barton-upon-Humber 103–104
Bead Stringing icebreaker 70
Bean Counter tool 128–129, *129*
Beany Counters 100
behaviours and attitudes, PAR process 55–57
benefit sharing (Indigenous research ethical principle) 140
bias, in generative AI technologies 9–10
Big Local funding 38
'big shifts' in PAR 43, **43**
  from closed to open enquiry 50
  from extracting to empowering 49
  from individual to group perspectives 54–55
  from teaching to facilitating 43–46, **44**
  from text-based to visual and verbal approaches 50–54

Index

from top-down to bottom-up 46–49
'Big Society' agenda 33
'Bike Rack' technique 71–72, 115
Black African researchers 47
Black storytelling 26
Boal, Augusto 71
body maps 75, 100, *106*, 107–109
bottom-up approaches, 'big shift' from top-down approaches to 46–49
British Red Cross PAR project 67
Brown Bag Lunch, Aberfeldy estate 85
Brydon-Miller, M. 138

C

California Institute for Women 25
Camden, London 33, 48–49
Camden Council 80–81
Cameron, David 33
carousel tool 76
Castleford 34
Causal Impact Diagrams 100, *119*, 119–121
celebration events 84–85, 131, 151
Centre for Community Studies 38
Centre for Lifelong Learning, University of Hull 29
Centre for Social Justice and Community Action 137–138
Chambers, Robert 21, 22–23, 24, 27, 28, 43, 55, 69, 99, 123, 137
change 3
 action for 5–6
 client-driven projects 87–88
 lack of 152
Children's Centres 28
Chilisa, Bagele 21, 25–26, 40, 140
citizen researchers *see* community researchers
citizen science maps 102
Clarke, Yaya 19
client-driven projects, enacting change 87–88
client-led tours 72–73
closed enquiry, 'big shift' to open enquiry 50
clustering, workshop design techniques 75–76
co-production 11, 37
Coalition government, austerity policies 32–33, 36, 41

collage 51
commissioning/commissioners 4, 16, 18, 50, 59, 61–62, 64, 66, 85, 88, 96–97
 commissioner briefing 72–73
 ethical guidelines 138
 guidance for 138, 158
 pitfalls and strategies 143, 146, 153, 154
communication skills 64
communities
 empowerment of 5, 23, 29, 31, 48, 55, 88, 90, 136
community asset/hazard maps 102
community champions 96–97
Community Development Company 153
Community Development Foundation 32
community-driven projects, enacting change 87–91
Community Insights Programme, Tower Hamlets 94–95
Community Matters 32
community of knowledge (Indigenous research ethical principle) 140
Community Research Hubs, UKRI (UK Research and Innovation) 10
Community Researcher Networks, UKRI (UK Research and Innovation) 38
community researchers 3–4, 5
 and Arnstein 18, 20–21
 benefits of collaboration with 4–6
 empowerment of 19, 24, 60, 68, 131, 143, 144, 148–149, 150–151
 facilitation skills 75, 80–81
 follow-up opportunities and career development 66–68, 154–155
 and Freire 19
 as gatekeepers 144
 and Lewin 20
 pay and remuneration issues 39–40, 64–66, 152–154
 recruitment of 2, 61–64
 skills and competencies 64
 structure and support issues 148–149
 support of relationships with 151–152

team roles 74–75
training of 2, 7, 13
  body maps 108
  London 33–34
  preparation stage of PAR 68–76
  time constraints 145–146
  Timelines 111–112
  Yorkshire 28–29
  see also peer researchers
'concientizacao' (critical consciousness) (Freire) 12–13
confidence, participatory behaviour 56
Consensus Workshop methodology, ICA (Institute for Cultural Affairs) 124, 126
Cooke, B. 24
Creative Acts for Curious People (Greenberg) 71
creative methods 3, 4, 85–86, 162
  see also arts, the
Criteria Ranking 100, 129, *129*
Crome, Susie 61
CSJCA (Centre for Social Justice and Community Action), Durham University 35–36
cultural maps 101
'culture of poverty' 30–31
curiosity, community researcher skills and competencies 64

D

data analysis *see* analysis
data collection 3, 4, 7, 54, 81, 152
  see also fieldwork
Decolonizing Methodologies (Tuhiwai Smith) 21, 25, 26
deindustrialisation 30–31
Design Council 83
  Framework for Innovation 123
  Methods Bank 123
Designmine 123
Development Agency for Yorkshire and the Humber 29
diagramming methodologies 4, 51
  see also visual methodologies
disability, people with 136, 139
  and mapping 105–106
dominators 149–150
drawing methodologies 4, 51
  see also visual methodologies
Duffy, Liz 141–142

Dulwich Picture Gallery, Past for the Present project 19, 51–54, 79, 93–94
Durham University, CSJCA (Centre for Social Justice and Community Action) 35–36

E

East Riding of Yorkshire 1, 28–31
Economic and Social Research Council, 'Framework for research ethics' 66
education
  and Freire 12–14
  see also teaching; training
embedded evaluation 92–93
empowerment 41
  and Arnstein 20
  'big shift' from extracting to 49
  of communities 5, 23, 29, 31, 48, 55, 88, 90, 136
  community researchers 5, 148–149
  of community researchers 19, 24, 60, 68, 131, 143, 144, 148–149, 150–151
  and Freire 13, 14, 19
  of participants 72, 107, 110, 112, 161
enthusiasm, community researcher skills and competencies 64
errors, embracing of 56
ethical issues 8, 16, 39, 136–137, 142, 159
  community-researcher-led ethics 141–142
  CSJCA (Centre for Social Justice and Community Action) guidelines 35
  Economic and Social Research Council 'Framework for research ethics' 66
  ethical standards 137–138
  'everyday ethics' 138–139
  Indigenous research ethics 140, 161
  Social Research Association 'Ethical guidelines' 66
  and vulnerability 139–140
ethnicity, and mapping 105–106
Euro-centric research 21, 160–161
  generative AI technologies 10
European Citizen Science Association 38

Index

Evaluation Betty 76, 92, 100–101, *132*, 132–134
evaluation (PAR process stage) 92, 152
  embedded evaluation 92–93
  independent evaluators 93–94
  PAR as an evaluation tool 96–97
  systematic evaluation 94–96
evaluation tools 76, 100–101, 131–132
  Evaluation Betty 76, 92, 100–101, *132*, 132–134
  Head, Heart, Bag, Bin tool 132, 133
  Pizza Pie (Evaluation Wheel) 76, 92, 100–101, *134*, 134–135
Evaluation Wheel (Pizza Pie) 76, 92, 100–101, *134*, 134–135
evidence-based policy 9
exploration tools 100, 101
  Graffiti Walls 100, 113–116, *114*
  mapping 51, 77, 100, 101–106, *103*
    body maps 75, 100, *106*, 107–109
  Timelines 82, 100, 109–113, *110*
extended collaborative projects 91–92
extracting, 'big shift' to empowering 49

F

facilitating, 'big shift' from teaching to 43–46, **44**
facilitators 18
  Facilitator role 74
  trainer/facilitator wellbeing failures 155–158
feedback tools 84–85
  body maps 108
feminism 21, 22, 25, 26–27, 41, 46, 160
fieldwork 77–82
  Causal Impact Diagrams 100, *119*, 120–121
  design of 3
  Graffiti Walls 100, *114*, 115–116
  H-Forms 81, 82, 92, 100, 116–119, *117*
  and mapping 106
  Rose-Bud-Thorn and Affinity Clustering tools 81–82, 92, *124*, 124–125, 126–127

time constraints 146
Timelines 82, 100, 109–113, *110*
financial crash, 2008 32–33, 41
fishbone diagrams 120
flexibility, participatory behaviour 56
Flower, Charlotte 29
focused discussion tools 100, 116
  Causal Impact Diagram 100, *119*, 119–121
  H-Form 81, 82, 100, 116–119, *117*
  Spider Diagram 100, 119, 121–122, *123*
Freire, Paulo 11, 12–14, 41, 43
  and community researchers 19
Futurejobs project, Hastings 34

G

gallery walls 76
Games for Actors and Non-actors (Boal) 71
gatekeepers
  community researcher recruitment 63
  professionals' power and gatekeeping issues 143–144
gender
  and mapping 105–106
  see also women
generative AI technologies 9–10
GIS (geographic information systems) 102
Gooda, Theresa 85–87
Graffiti Walls 100, 113–116, *114*
green space project 90–91
Greenberg, Sarah Stein 71
group perspectives, 'big shift' from individual perspectives to 54–55
'Guidance on Payment for Public Partners' (UKRI) 65–66

H

H-Forms 81, 82, 92, 100, 116–119, *117*
Hanington, B. 125
HARCA (Poplar Housing and Regeneration Community Association) 34
Harkness, Fran 158
Hartlepool Action Lab 35
Harwood studies (Lewin) 15–16

Hastings 34
Hay, Rowena 158
Head, Heart, Bag, Bin tool 132, 133
health equity maps 102
HEYPAN (Hull and East Yorkshire Participatory Appraisal Network) 28, 29, 33
historical maps 102
Holdsworth, Gina 160
Home Office, Active Communities Unit 32
honesty, participatory behaviour 56
Housing Action Trusts 28
housing association project, East London 88
Hoyle, Sarah 84
Hull, UK 1, 2, 28–31, 160
Hull and East Yorkshire Participatory Appraisal Network (HEYPAN) 28, 29, 33
Hull City Vision 28
Humber and Wolds Community Council 103–104

I

ICA (Institute for Cultural Affairs)
  Consensus Workshop methodology 124, 126
  Technology of Participation 123–124
icebreakers 70–71, 106, 147
IDEO 123
Impact Criteria 128
Impact Matrix 128, 129–131, *130*
inclusion 27, 45, 69, 138
independent evaluators 93–94
independent PAR
  practitioners 33–34
  wellbeing and remuneration issues 155–158, 160
  see also professionals
India, NGOs 23
Indigenous critique of PAR 21, 22, 25–27, 161
Indigenous research ethics 140, 161
Indigenous Research Methodologies (Chilisa) 21, 25–26, 140
individual perspectives, 'big shift' to group perspectives 54–55
industrial organisations, Lewin's research in 15–16
information sharing 150–151
  see also research findings

Inglis, Andy 27, 28–29, 116
'Ingredients for Terrible Teams' exercise 71–72
'insider view' of community researchers 4–6
Institute of Development Studies, University of Sussex 27, 29
International Collaboration for Participatory Health Research 35
international development, and PAR 21–23, 41, 160
participation 'tyranny' criticism 23–24

J

John Moores University 155
Joseph, Christiana 82
JRF (Joseph Rowntree Foundation) 24–25
  Neighbourhood Approaches to Loneliness Programme 89–90, 132
Jusic, Ada 84

K

Kamal, Kohenoor 84
Kapoor, I. 24–25
Kar, Kamal 21
Kara, Helen 140, 155, 157
Kawakita, Jiro 125
Kesby, M. 87
Key Moments icebreaker 70
Khalil, Anita 33, 80–81
Kindon, S.L. 87
Kothari, U. 24

L

'Ladder of Participation' (Arnstein) 16–18, 43
Lavithis, Niki 19
learning
  different needs in 45
  participatory behaviour 55
Lewin, Kurt 11, 14–17, 41, 42, 57
  and community researchers 20
LGBTQ+ communities 136
Liberating Structures 71
Limehouse, East London 113
linguistic maps 102
listening
  community researcher skills and competencies 64
  participatory behaviour 55

Index

listing, workshop design technique 75–76
living wage 65
  see also pay and remuneration
local knowledge 77–78
  community researcher skills and competencies 64
Local Trust 38
  Big Local programme 10
Ludlow, Barbara 33

M

Mackie, Nathan 19
mapping 51, 77, 100 101–106, *103*
  body maps 75, 100, *106*, 107–109
marginalised groups 144, 161
  power relations and PAR 136
  vulnerability and ethics 139–140
Martin, B. 125
maternity care
  positionality issues 47
  UCL's Partners Better Births project 91–92
Matrix Ranking 100
McCarroll, Clare 133
Mead, Margaret 15
metaphors, in mapping exercises 105
Mexican American Research Association 25
Michalko, Michael 71
Miettinen, S. 26
Mighty Mini Research Collective 157, 158
mobility maps 102
Model Cities programme 17
Molina, Jo 19
Morris, Celia 19
Munck, R. 24
music, and research findings 51–54

N

National Coordinating Centre for Public Engagement 138
National Lottery funding 29
National Trust 85–87
neutrality, participatory behaviour 55
New Deal for Communities 28, 30
New Labour, community policies 28–30
Newman, K. 93
Newton, Roger 132
Northumbria University, PeaNut 29

O

Observer role 74–75
occupation, and mapping 105–106
Okeke, Tara 19
open-ended questions 60
open enquiry, 'big shift' from closed enquiry to 50
Oxfam, UK Poverty Programme 29
  PPfC (Participatory Practitioners for Action) 28

P

PA (Participatory Appraisal) 119, 123, 127
  Hull and the East Riding of Yorkshire, UK 27–32
Pain, R. 87
Pala, Achola 25
PAR (Participatory Action Research) 3–4
  benefits of community researcher collaboration 4–6
  challenges of 3, 61, 143–158
  current context 36–41
  history and development of 7, 10–11, 41
    feminist, postcolonial and Indigenous critiques of 21, 22, 24–27, 41
    foundational figures 11–21
    UK 27–34
    independent practitioner-led work 33–34
    institutional support for 34–36
    international development 21–27, 41
  magic of 61
  pitfalls and strategies 137
    discontinuity of projects 154–155
    dominators and saboteurs 149–150
    hoarding data/insights 150–151
    inadequate structure/support 148–149
    lack of tangible change 152
    pay and remuneration issues 152–154, 157–158
    perfectionism 149
    professional power/gatekeeping 143–144
    professionals who 'already know it all' 151–152

restrictive research questions 143
status and power
symbols 146–148
time constraints 144–146
trainer/facilitator wellbeing
failures 155–158
potential traps in projects 31–32
risks facing 11
scope of in UK 6–7
sustaining practice of 160–162
PAR (Participatory Action
Research) methodologies 37
PAR (Participatory Action
Research) process 42, 57, *58*,
97–98, 161
action 84–92
ethos and approach 42–57, **43,
44**
evaluation 92–97
partnering 59–68, *60*
preparation 68–76
research 76–84
PAR (Participatory Action
Research) tools 7, 67, 99–100,
135, 161, 162
action planning tools 100, 127–
131, *128*, *129*, *130*
analysis tools 100, 123–127,
124, *125*
evaluation tools 100–101,
131–135, *132*, *134*
exploration tools *1–3*, 100,
101–116, *106*, *110*, *114*
focused discussion tools 100,
116–122
tool sequencing 100–101
Parent Council 33
Parent Council, Camden 48–49
Parker, Priya 69
Participation: The New Tyranny
(Cooke and Kothari) 24
Participatory Learning and Action
(PLA) 23, 119–120, 123,
127, 136
Participatory Practitioners for Action
(PPfC), Oxfam 28
Participatory Practitioners for
Change 138
Participatory Research Innovation
and Learning Labs 36
Participatory Rural Appraisal
(PRA) 23, 127, 136
participatory video 51

partnering (PAR process
stage) *58*, 59
checklist for vetting projects and
partnerships 59, *60*
collaborative brief
development 59–61
community researcher career
opportunities and legacy 66–68
community researcher pay and
terms 39–40, 64–66, 152–154
community researcher
recruitment 61–64
past experiences 61
Patient Involvement Partners,
UCL's Partners Better Births
project 91–92
pay and remuneration
community researchers 39–40,
64–66, 152–154
independent PAR
practitioners 157–158
Peabody College, Vanderbilt
University, US 68
Pedagogy of the Oppressed
(Freire) 13–14
peer researchers 7, 10, 28, 38, 57,
63, 138
see also community researchers
Perrin, Calum 19, 51–54
Petworth Detectives 77–78
Petworth House 85–87
photovoice 3, 51
Pizza Pie (Evaluation Wheel) 76,
92, 100–101, *134*, 134–135
PLA (Participatory Learning and
Action) 23, 119–120, 123,
127, 136
place maps 103, *103*
Poplar Housing and Regeneration
Community Association
(HARCA) 34
positionality
data analysis 83
maternity care research 47
Positive Action Recruitment
Roadmap 63
postcolonial critique of PAR 21, 22,
24–25, 26–27, 41, 160
potential/ideal maps 102
power issues 8, 11, 14, 136–137,
159
and community researchers 4
'Ladder of Participation' 16–18

participatory behaviour 55
pitfalls and strategies 137
 discontinuity of projects 154–155
 dominators and saboteurs 149–150
 hoarding data/insights 150–151
 inadequate structure/support 148–149
 lack of tangible change 152
 pay and renumeration issues 39–40, 152–154, 157–158
 perfectionism 149
 professional power/gatekeeping 143–144
 professionals who 'already know it all' 151–152
 restrictive research questions 143
 status and power symbols 146–148
 time constraints 144–146
 trainer/facilitator wellbeing failures 155–158
 research teams 55
power maps 102
PowerPoint, avoidance of 148
PPfC (Participatory Practitioners for Action), Oxfam 28
PRA (Participatory Rural Appraisal) 23, 127, 136
praxis (Freire) 13
preconceptions
 participatory behaviour 55
preparation (PAR process stage) *58*, 68–69
 client/commissioner briefing 72–73
 Graffiti Walls 100, 113–116, *114*
 ground rules and 'Bike Rack' technique 71–72
 icebreakers 70–71
 participatory approach in 69–70
 starting research 74
 team roles 74–75
 Timelines 82, 100, 109–113, *110*
 workshop design techniques 75–76
press, local 31
problem tree diagrams 120
professionals
 power and gatekeeping issues 143–144
 status and power symbols 146–148
 who 'already know it all' 151–152

see also independent PAR practitioners
project constraints 60
Providence Row 34
Puri, Radhika 96–97
Putting the Last First (Chambers) 22–23

Q

Quaker Social Action, *Head, Heart, Bag, Bin* tool 132, 133
qualitative research 3, 4, 9–10
quantitative research 3, 9
Question Bank 73, 77, 81, 99

R

racism 35
 Black African researchers 47
ranking and scoring tools 127–131, *128*, *129*
Rapid Rural Appraisal (RRA) 23, 119
rapport
 participatory behaviour 55
 preparation (PAR process stage) 73
reciprocity (Indigenous research ethical principle) 140
recommendations, definition of 3
REF (Research Excellence Framework) 37
reflection
 community researcher training 69, 112
 fieldwork 81–82
 reflective journaling 55
 workshop design techniques 75
Reflective Timeline 92
reflexivity 45, 47
refugees 7, 105, 136
Regional Development Agencies 28, 32
relational accountability (Indigenous research ethical principle) 140
research briefs, collaborative brief development 59–61
research commissioners *see* commissioning/commissioners
research design 4, 77–81
 collaborative question development 143
Research England, Participatory Research Funding 37

Research Excellence Framework (REF) 37
research findings 82–84
  creative approaches 51–54, 151
  hoarding of data and insights 150–151
  reporting and feedback 84–87, 151
  sharing of 3, 4, 150–151
  see also analysis
research objectives, preparation (PAR process stage) 73
research (PAR process stage) 76–77
  data analysis and reporting 82–84
  fieldwork 77–82
  research design 4, 77–81
research teams
  diversity in 54–55
  power issues 55
  roles and responsibilities 60, 74–75
  team size and composition 157
respect
  community researcher skills and competencies 64
  participatory behaviour 55
Rezvani, Sohrab 141–142
role playing 55
Rose-Bud-Thorn tool 81–82, 92, *124*, 124–125, 126
RRA (Rapid Rural Appraisal) 23, 119
Rubalcava, Magdalen 19
'Rugby Post Form' *see* H-Form
rural areas 77–78
  Rapid Rural Appraisal (RRA) 23, 119
  rural development, and PAR 22–23
Ryan, F. 139

S

saboteurs 149–150
  'anti-saboteur' measures 31, 75, 108, 150
Sarantou, M. 26
scenario planning 55
School of Social Entrepreneurs 157
Seed Mixer icebreaker 70
self-awareness, participatory behaviour 56
self-reflection
  Action Research 15
  participatory behaviour 56
  see also reflection; reflexivity

Sellers, Tilly 28
Seppälä, T. 26
SHAK (South Hampstead Community Centre) 33
sharing, participatory behaviour 56
Single Regeneration Budget (SRB) 28, 29, 153
Smile Sharing icebreaker 70
social leadership, body maps 108–109
social maps 101
Social Research Association, 'Ethical guidelines' 66
SOS Gangs Project, St Giles Trust 34, 112, 113
Soteriou, Sandra 33
Sourcebook of Ideas and Activities for Participatory Workshops, A (Chambers) 137
South Hampstead Community Centre (SHAK) 33
South Tyneside 56–57
Spider Diagrams 100, 119, 121–122, *123*
SRB (Single Regeneration Budget) 28, 29, 153
St Giles Trust, SOS Gangs Project 34, 112, 113
stakeholders
  stakeholder mapping 61
  support of relationships with 151–152
stereotypes
  Black African researchers 47
  generative AI technologies 9–10
strong opinions, participatory behaviour 56–57
support
  community researchers structure and support issues 148–149
  support of relationships with 151–152
  participatory behaviour 56
systematic evaluation 94–96

T

Tate, Susan 77–78
teaching
  'big shift' to facilitating 43–46, **44**
  teaching and learning cycles 76
  see also education; training
teams *see* research teams

Technology of Participation, ICA (Institute for Cultural Affairs) 123–124
Templeton, Alis 93–94
text-based approaches, 'big shift' to visual and verbal approaches 50–54
theatre 51
Thinkertoys: A Handbook of Creative-Thinking Techniques (Michalko) 71
time constraints 144–146
Timelines 82, 100, 109–113, *110*
Todmorden 34
Toliver, S.R. 26
tools *see* PAR (Participatory Action Research) tools
top-down approaches, 'big shift' to bottom-up approaches 46–49
Tower Hamlets, London 33–34
  Community Insights Programme 94–95
  Health Trainers programme 96–97
Tower Hamlets Public Health 61, 96–97
Toynbee Halls 34
trainers/facilitators, wellbeing issues 155–158
training 2, 7, 13
  body maps 108
  London 33–34
  preparation stage of PAR 68–76
  time constraints 145–146
  Timelines 111–112
  Yorkshire 28–29
Tuhiwai Smith, L. 21, 25, 26

U

UCL's Partners Better Births project 91–92
UK Forum for Independent Researchers 157
UK Participatory Research Network 36
UKRI (UK Research and Innovation)
  Community Research Hubs 10

Community Researcher Networks 38
'Guidance on Payment for Public Partners' 65–66
University of Hull, Centre for Lifelong Learning 29
University of Sussex, Institute of Development Studies 27, 29

V

verbal approaches, 'big shift' from text-based approaches to 50–54
visual methodologies 4, 84
  'big shift' from text-based approaches to 50–54
  RRA (Rapid Rural Appraisal) 23
  vulnerability and ethics 139
  see also diagramming methodologies; drawing methodologies
Vowden, Imogen 82
vulnerability 161
  and ethics 139–140

W

Wakefield 34
watching, participatory behaviour 55
Weber-Pillwax, C. 140
welfare benefits 65
Westerby, Martin 33
Western-centric research 21, 160–161
  generative AI technologies 10
women 136
  vulnerability and ethics 139
working-class communities 30–31, 136

Y

Yorkshire Forward 28, 29
Young Foundation 10, 38, 138
Your Need to Know Campaign 82

Z

Zip! Zap! Pow! icebreaker 70–71

www.ingramcontent.com/pod-product-compliance
Lightning Source LLC
Chambersburg PA
CBHW051544020426
42333CB00016B/2087